Contemplative Qualitative Inquiry

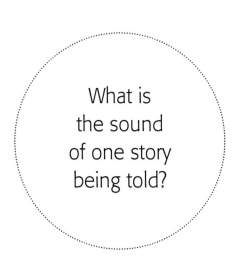

What is
the sound
of one story
being told?

Contemplative
Qualitative Inquiry

Practicing the Zen of Research

Valerie J. Janesick

 Routledge
Taylor & Francis Group

LONDON AND NEW YORK

First published 2015 by Left Coast Press, Inc.

Published 2016 by Routledge
2 Park Square, Milton Park, Abingdon, Oxon OX14 4RN
711 Third Avenue, New York, NY 10017, USA

Routledge is an imprint of the Taylor & Francis Group, an informa business

ISBN 978-1-61132-955-1 hardcover
ISBN 978-1-61132-956-8 paperback

Library of Congress Cataloging-in-Publication Data

Janesick, Valerie J.
  Contemplative qualitative inquiry : practicing the Zen of research / Valerie J. Janesick.
    pages cm
  Includes bibliographical references.
  ISBN 978-1-61132-955-1 (hardback) -- ISBN 978-1-61132-956-8 (paperback) -- ISBN 978-1-61132-761-8 (consumer ebook)
  1. Qualitative research. 2. Social sciences--Research--Methodology. 3. Zen Buddhism. 4. Creative ability--Religious aspects--Buddhism. I. Title.
  H62.J3457 2015
  001.4'2--dc23
                          2014047052

 **CONTENTS**

APPENDICES

This book is dedicated to the memory of
Elliot W. Eisner
*and to all who think outside the box
and continue to model a mindful approach
to research and to life.*

 **PREFACE**

I am sitting in a yoga studio and learning the practice of Zen mantra-based meditation during a beginners' meditation class. It is the summer of 1971 in Ann Arbor, Michigan. It is a calm and sunny day with sunlight streaming into the studio. The teacher has practiced Zen meditation over a lifetime of sixty years and begins with a Zen koan about a cup of tea.

> Nan-in, a Japanese teacher, received a university professor who came to inquire about Zen. Nan-in served tea. He poured his visitor's cup full, and then kept on pouring. The professor watched the overflow until he no longer could restrain himself. "It is overfull. No more will go in!"
> "Like this cup," Nan-in said, "you are full of your own opinions and speculations. How can I show you Zen unless you first empty your cup?"
>
> *Empty Cup koan*

I recall thinking that this idea was something I wanted to write about someday in terms of qualitative research. Like emptying the teacup, to do a qualitative research project it is always good to empty your mind of the previously held notions about research. I had just completed a Master's thesis in qualitative research and was struck by the similarities between qualitative research methods and the philosophy and practice of Zen Buddhism.

Zen koans present a question with the answer imbedded in the question. The question is usually posed by a student, who asks a teacher the question. Bear in mind that in the Asian tradition teachers are revered. It is part of the Asian culture to learn from a teacher and to

Valerie J. Janesick, "Preface" in *Contemplative Qualitative Inquiry: Practicing the Zen of Research*, pp. 11-17. © 2015 Left Coast Press, Inc. All rights reserved.

follow in a tradition. I was always struck by the koan nature of constructing good questions for research interviewing. Thus, another reason to write about this topic became clear. Throughout this book I will be posing questions in the style of the teacher of meditation. Also, each section will begin with a Zen koan, or riddle-like story, and will end with a sutra, or Zen teaching.

Fast forward to Chicago in the spring of 2007. I am sitting in a yoga studio practicing Zen mantra-based meditation prior to a yoga class, and am planning to attend a research conference later that day. The studio is utterly silent this morning. Although it is a cloudy and windy day, the studio is positioned so that, this morning, a ray of sunlight comes through in a diagonal line ending at the feet of the instructor, who is seated in the lotus position. There is a beautiful, calm feeling. The teacher begins the class saying that she doesn't actually teach meditation or yoga, all she does is research. It was then I knew that it was time to write this book about contemplative qualitative inquiry and the practice of Zen in research. She starts the class reading a Haiku poem. All at once I recall a high school English class where we were studying and writing not only Haiku but other Japanese forms of poetry as well. I remember, at that moment, that it was, indeed, haiku that got me interested in meditation and yoga in the first place. I then went to the conference and spoke to Mitch Allen, who reminded me of a conversation we had in the 1990s. Mitch was the editor for the first edition of my first book *Stretching Exercises for Qualitative Researchers* and was, at that time, working for Sage Publications. He asked me, "What would you like to do next?" I said that I'd always wanted to do a book that combines Zen and qualitative research with a title in that vein. He encouraged me and now, finally, after all these years, I am sitting down to put these ideas together.

Following presentations at conferences, and even after classes, many individuals have asked me how long it takes to write a book. I promised them that in the next book I wrote, and all books thereafter, I would include a statement describing how the book came to be, from start to finish. In order to talk about this, I need to tell you a story.

Recently, all faculty at my institution were asked to take an online course on how to teach online. Presumably one of the unstated goals was to get more faculty to teach online, assuming that students today want online classes. One of the assignments in the course was to join a free massive open online course (MOOC), to experience it, and then to reflect on it. I joined a course titled "How to Write a Book in Two Weeks," in which over 600 persons were enrolled. Since I have never known anyone who wrote a book in two weeks and I personally have never written a book in two weeks, this being my eighth book, I joined the class. I was curious, and wondered who writes a book in two weeks, what kind of book and under what conditions. I suspect that many in the class had similar curiosities and may have been considering writing a book.

The first requirement of the MOOC was to tell the instructor and the 600 plus participants why I had enrolled in this free course. I mentioned that the title intrigued me due to the fact that, at the very least, a time span of a few years or decades to write a book was normal for me and that my curiosity was sparked when I saw the MOOC title. I then mentioned that enrolling in a MOOC was a requirement for an online course I was taking. I also explained that, in looking over what I had written, I saw that there was, first, a saturation-in-thought period before I composed a prospectus for a book; second, a reading and research period, which might take years; third, the actual writing period; and, fourth, finally, the rewriting, proofing, and editing period. I am not sure how this statement was interpreted, but this explanation occurred at the time that I wrote the prospectus for this book, *Contemplative Qualitative Inquiry: Practicing the Zen of Research*. As a result, I decided to track the time that it took to write this book.

I see writing a book as a developmental undertaking. In terms of first thinking about it, this book began in the 1970s, which was before I began doctoral studies and before I focused my academic interest on research methods, particularly qualitative research methods. I put the idea aside, however, as other projects came along. When I started my career and began teaching qualitative methods classes, then as an assistant professor at the State University of New York in Albany, I had just finished a qualitative dissertation. My reading and research period started then, but it continues to the present. I also started taking yoga and meditation classes at various Zen or yoga centers, a practice that has continued throughout my life. As well, I kept a yoga and meditation journal. As in writing any book, article or book chapter, I routinely made notes and wrote down any apt phrases or quotations that I came across, assuming that I would use them eventually.

For this book, I sent in the signed publication agreement by email in May 2013, upon having the prospectus accepted. While preparing the outline for the book, which by the way changed completely as I got into the writing, I wrote a section or two from time to time. Some of my commitments for chapters for handbooks and other books had deadlines ahead of this book, and so I concentrated on them, all the while taking notes as I came across resources, websites, list serves, and new books related to this topic. Left Coast Press, Inc. is a caring and compassionate organization and I have been given a few extensions, but I sent in the manuscript in final form in October 2014. So, seventeen months have passed since I signed the agreement and began the actual writing. In addition, the prospectus took a few months prior to the writing, as I thought about the book, wrote notes, and rewrote the outline. I also spent a great deal of time at the end rewriting, changing chapter titles, changing information, and deleting excess material. This past summer, from July 5th to August 18th, I wrote for four to five hours every day. After receiving feedback from my editor, I wrote as often as possible from September 8th to the 30th between classes and meetings. From October 1st to the 30th, I wrote for approximately six hours per day on the weekend and two hours per day twice during the week. I always start writing in the morning, as early as possible. I got into this habit through journal writing every morning as part of yoga practice. Coincidentally, since the year 2000, I have taken a number of workshops through the Chicago Yoga Center at various sites, with the Chopra Center, and with Lama Surya Das. The two books that influenced me the most were *The Seven Spiritual Laws of Yoga* by Deepak Chopra and David Simon and *Awakening the Buddha Within* by Lama Surya Das. These books are classics, and can assist in broadening awareness about meditation and yoga. I mention them because through reading about meditation, layers of understanding pop up when you least expect them. These books had a profound effect on my thinking, writing, and rewriting.

Basically, this book evolved over forty years or more. Deadlines are wonderful things! This is the process I have followed in the books I have written and rewritten. My next project will most likely follow a similar time frame and plan.

With that said, now I am going to ask you not to read this book. Rather than reading the book, I want you to *experience* it. Not only that, I want to introduce the metaphor of thinking with a Zen mindset in your approach to this experience. There are many books, articles, videos, websites, and CDs about Zen Buddhism and meditation, and there are many types of Buddhism, most of which are offshoots of Zen. This book, however, is not about Buddhism. It is about using the metaphor of Zen to reflect on qualitative research techniques, processes, and overall concepts. For this book, I am focusing on three key, big-picture aspects of Zen that most writers in this arena agree upon, and I have organized the book around these three qualities. Many writers have written elegantly about these qualities, each in their own way, and they are in agreement, no matter what words are used to describe these qualities. Hanh (2001), for example, captures these qualities of Buddhism in a way that helped me to organize this manuscript. He is a well established Vietnamese Buddhist monk, teacher, and writer living in France and teaching around the globe. These three aspects that capture the essence of Zen are *impermanence, non-self,* and *nirvana.*

Impermanence, Non-Self, and Nirvana

Impermanence, non-self, and nirvana are facets of Zen that are the organizing architecture for this book. Impermanence is a cornerstone of Zen, and is an accurate term for this major tenet of Buddhism. Many writers claim that if you want to understand Buddhism, just remember that everything changes. Thus the notion of impermanence. In our fast paced, cluttered world we often fall into a mindset that expects things not to change. As I learned more about Zen, I couldn't help but wonder at the connections between impermanence and the fact that all findings are tentative in any research project and most certainly in qualitative research projects.

Likewise, the idea of non-self appears in every part of writing and practice of Zen. The notion of impermanence leads us to non-self. When you look deeply into yourself, you see that you already have everything within you. This idea is sometimes referred to in Zen practice as the mystery of inter-being, or the one contains everything. It is a strong notion from the East and often difficult for Western thinkers to comprehend. Essentially, non-self means that there is no such thing as separate existence. We exist in the universe connected to others. Again, I couldn't help but wonder at the resonance of this notion with qualitative work, where the researcher is the research instrument. How much more connected can one get to a research project?

Finally, the notion of nirvana, which is about coming to peace with the universe as it is in the present, is the third major quality of the essence of Zen. Nirvana is the extinction of all concepts and all pain through to the realization that there is no need to fear suffering since we have all manifestations of life within us. Our ancestors are in us. The people in our lives are also with us. Eventually, we become the ancestors. Thus, nirvana becomes a powerful way to understand the importance of the Zen mind. Extending this thinking to qualitative research projects, when the researcher and research participant/s are in complete understanding, one might say that nirvana has been achieved. My meditation teachers would call this achievement a "violent clarity." This clarity should be effortless and inclusive of the world, which is the reason why some writers equate nirvana with a state of bliss. In Zen thinking, the self is an illusion, and when that concept is realized, all is bliss. Likewise, nirvana, like all facets of Zen, implies living in the present moment. For qualitative researchers this idea also makes sense. We live in the present moment during the qualitative research process.

Throughout this book, I connect these powerful ideas to qualitative research theories, methodology, and practice. Each chapter contains two kinds of exercises that I call *mindful activities* and *mindful moments*, as well as suggested resources for further understanding the concepts discussed in that chapter. *Sutras* are included as well. One chapter focuses on poetry in Zen and its applications in qualitative research for writing *found data poems* and *identity poetry*. Related to all of our practice is the chapter on the *researcher reflective journal*. The book closes with a chapter on *satori*, the Japanese word for understanding, using the title Satori, Zenergy, Analysis, and Understanding. *Zenergy* is my term for Zen energy. Meditation produces an amazing amount of mind energy, which is exceedingly useful to the qualitative researcher. Thus the term zenergy was born. All of this provides a new way of moving toward understanding our work as well as our participants' lives.

This book affords a way of honoring my meditation teachers/ancestors and my research methods teachers/ancestors. Since Buddhism originally came to the West from books, it is fitting that a book be written to extend this tradition to applied research. I hope that this book will expand the rich tradition of qualitative research methodology to include looking to the East for inspiration, in this case to Zen. I use Zen in its widest and most inclusive sense. Throughout the book, I connect the Zen mind to the qualitative research mind. May this book be helpful, useful, and meaningful to both emerging and advanced members of our research community. It is not meant to be prescriptive or authoritative but simply a thought provoking way of noticing something or seeing the world in a new way. Since Zen covers the natural and the spiritual and since qualitative researchers are routinely looking for ways to improve our inner and outer practices, I hope this book can contribute to our field of research in some small way and in the present moment.

Acknowledgments

Writing a book like this, outside the box of traditional approaches to research methods, requires that trust is established between the author and publisher. I am grateful to Mitch Allen and the entire crew of Left Coast Press, Inc. I am also grateful to the staff at Mojo's Used Books and Records Café in Tampa, my favorite place for proofing and revising my daily writing on this book. Everyone there was always encouraging and welcoming. As always, I am grateful to my teachers at the Chicago Yoga Center, especially Suddha Weixler and Dale Morphew at the now former Tampa Yoga Café. They helped me through their insight and creativity. I am grateful to my teachers at the Chopra Center, especially Deepak Chopra and the late David Simon, and to Lama Surya Das, whose writings, workshops, and website are always inspiring. Finally, I am grateful to Sakarai Sensei, our host professor for a Fulbright scholar exchange, for planning a trip to Kyoto to experience Japan. Aregato, Sensei!

Valerie J. Janesick
Tampa, Florida
October 2014

CHAPTER ONE

About Zen and Contemplative Inquiry

A monk asked Chimon, "Before the lotus blossom emerged from the water, what is it?" Chimon replied, "A lotus blossom." The monk persevered, "After it has come out of the water, what is it?" Chimon replied "Lotus leaves."

Lotus koan

Introduction

What is Zen? I define it as follows. Zen is a form of Buddhism that asserts that enlightenment can be attained through meditation, self-contemplation and intuition by following several principles. The Zen mind is a critical, meditative, and thoughtful mind. Zen relies on coming to know yourself and the world through meditation, which is called zazen. Here in the West, zazen is usually a combination of thirtyminutes of seated meditation facing a blank wall, with no distractions, and thirty minutes of walking meditation. This practice has been handed down for generations. Individuals who spend a great deal of the day meditating obviously elongate the process to a number of hours of both sitting and walking. Zen, which came from Asia, honors ancestry and the history of thought. A Zen student learns from a teacher, who learned from a teacher, etc., eventually becoming a teacher and extending the ancestral lineage of thinking. Thus the archeology of Zen helps to keep the memory and activity of the ancestry in process.

Valerie J. Janesick, "About Zen and Contemplative Inquiry" in *Contemplative Qualitative Inquiry: Practicing the Zen of Research*, pp. 19-39. © 2015 Left Coast Press, Inc. All rights reserved.

Using Zen as a metaphor, I see a way to approach qualitative research methods as contemplative inquiry. With this metaphor, we can move the field forward, as we more fully describe and explain impermanence, nonself, and nirvana. Likewise, Zen offers many koans, sutras or teachings, that help with the conduct of life. In this book, I use the concept of koans and sutras to add to our understanding of best practices of qualitative research in a mindful way. Mindfulness is important here, as it is a key goal of Zen practice. At the end of each chapter, I extend this notion to mindful activities and exercises. I use sutras about research in each chapter as well. Literally, in Sanskrit, *sutra* means a thread or line that holds something together. I borrow on that approach of holding things together with sutras about qualitative research techniques such as observation, interviewing, reflective journal writing, poetry, and document analysis. Finally, compassion figures prominently in Zen thinking. Do no harm to any living thing is a basic tenet of Zen. I see the resonance with our work, as qualitative researchers are compassionate in the sense of doing no harm. As well, an entire arm of bureaucracy in public and educational institutions, the Institutional Review Boards (IRBs), is dedicated to seeing that no harm, or at least minimal harm, is done in research settings.

Introducing Zen as a concept to frame qualitative research methods begins with a bit of history. Buddhism originated in India between the 6th and 4th centuries BCE. Zen is a school of Buddhism that began in China in the 6th century CE. The Chinese word Chan became Zen from its Japanese pronunciation. A number of Buddhist traditions have developed around the globe with slightly different emphases, but all agree in the most critical and fundamental ideas and thinking. From China, Buddhism spread to Japan, Korea, and Vietnam, and was adapted culturally to these countries.

Currently, Zen is practiced throughout the world. It is a way of thinking and for many represents a spiritual path. In that respect, you might think of Zen as a contemplative research method. I am focusing on the Zen tradition, because it is the tradition I am most familiar with and the one I continue to study. Zen uses storytelling, in that *koans* teach a lesson, from teacher to student, designed to provoke deeper thought. A koan is a type of riddle-like story, or thinking test. Zen also uses *sutras*, which are short bits or threads of wisdom and are also a type of storytelling. It is easy to see the connection between Zen and our work as qualitative researchers. Just as a Zen practitioner values the story, so do we value it in our research. After all the data are collected, we need to describe and interpret our participants' stories. Zen also offers us a way to view the world completely apart from our own Western culture. By bringing sensibilities from Eastern culture, we can open up new ways of thinking and writing. This approach calls to mind Albert Einstein's many statements that indicate that problems need to be addressed at a level of knowledge apart from the arena where they were created. Using Zen as a metaphor, we uncover new levels of awareness.

Zen also emphasizes *mindfulness*, which allows for enlightenment and insight into living. Mindfulness carries with it as well the notion of un-learning oppressive and harmful practices. The recently coined term anti-oppressive pedagogy resonates with Zen mindfulness, making the idea of Zen a powerful stimulus to thinking in a new, more expansive way. Zen has potential for influencing many fields, not the least of which is education. Certainly Zen has implications for research, and it is for this reason that I want to emphasize it as a way to understand and advance qualitative research projects. As mentioned in the Preface, Zen brings immediate awareness that impermanence is a fact of life. Everything changes. The capacity to realize and accept what impermanence means is in itself a big step in understanding Zen and in understanding qualitative research methods. Qualitative work allows for the impermanence of the social world: at any given moment things can and do change. Recently, after teaching advanced qualitative research classes, almost solely, I had the opportunity to teach a beginning qualitative methods class with eighteen students who were just beginning to understand research. What I learned from teaching beginners was that the beginner's mind asks the beginning questions, and until those questions are addressed, no progress can be made in the research project. Beginners often take the qualitative methods class as an afterthought, following three statistics classes, and so their questions are often framed as statistical methods questions. My job as a teacher is to help beginners to realize that they will be thinking in a new way and will have to give up previously held notions about research and posing research questions. The beginner's mind needs to be a clean mind. In Zen meditation, the beginner's mind is wiped clean of the self. Similarly, in qualitative research methodology, the beginner's mind is wiped clean of proving something, generalizing findings, or fitting them into a formula. Achieving a beginner's mind means giving up the idea of permanence. This is the first step in mindfulness, and it includes, at the least, an eagerness to live without oppressive behaviors.

In addition, *non-self,* that is, the realization that we are connected to people and the entire universe, is a powerful frame for understanding the theory and practice of qualitative research. Rather than thinking of the self, which is a delusion in Zen thinking, qualitative researchers think of being connected to the entire world through the participants in their studies. This idea resembles the notion of reflexivity and the ability to take on the perspectives of our participants. In other words, we are all participants in the research, struggling to make sense of our respective worlds. Finally, *nirvana,* which is the knowledge that we are one with and in the universe, can be useful here. The implication of nirvana is that the self is basically a delusion. How can there be a self, if each of us is connected to each other and to the universe? Again, we learn this powerful way of looking at the world from Eastern thinkers and writers. Once we are aware of our connections, we achieve a state of bliss, free of suffering. This practical concept is useful for those of us using qualitative methods to make sense of people's lives: we are connected to our participant/s whether or not we wish to be. I call this approach contemplative qualitative inquiry. The contemplative component has to do with the stillness and silence of thinking with a meditative orientation. It is my intention that this book begin a conversation about these ideas.

About Koans and Sutras

Frames that help to capture the spirit and meaning of Zen include koan practice and sutra lessons. Koans, or riddle-like stories, offer a way to use metaphor throughout daily life. Qualitative researchers use metaphor on a regular basis. Since a koan always teaches a lesson, there most certainly is resonance here with qualitative work. Comparably, a sutra is a short saying that refers to a lesson in life. Because they capture life moments, koans and sutras very much capture the essence of our work, since we also capture life moments. When used in qualitative work, they connect us to our history.

One of the most famous definitions of a sutra is itself a sutra in Indian literature, and is from the text *Vayu Purana,* as described by Mani (1975). "A sutra is: Of minimal syllabary, unambiguous, pithy, comprehensive, continuous, and without flaw; who knows the sutra knows it to be thus."

It is easy to see why a sutra can be useful and helpful to qualitative researchers. You might even think of creating sutras for your research. In the case of the koan, you will always find that the story contains a question and suggests an answer. This question is designed to give the student who asks the question the opportunity to go further in thinking. Following the Eastern tradition, the teacher does not answer the question before the student offers a response. In fact, the teacher often waits in silence to allow the learner to think through the question and to reflect on its meaning. Interestingly, the answer is most often embedded in the very question asked. As a result, research koans become a way to extend our practice, build theory, and answer conundrums. I am using Zen as a metaphor here, and purposely use it to capture the gist of qualitative research methods, all the while recalling the following words of the Chinese master painter and teacher Lu Ch'ai from the 1791 classic text on painting entitled *The Tao of Painting*:

> Some set great value on method, while others pride themselves on dispensing with method. To be without method is deplorable; but to depend on method entirely is worse. You must first learn to observe the rules faithfully; afterwards modify them according to your intelligence and capacity. The end of all method is to have no method. (Lu Ch'ai, 1791, as in Mai Mai, 1978)

In this wisdom lies the wisdom of Zen as well. For a person who practices Zen meditation and thinking, there is a calm associated with a mind free of method. Nevertheless, the path to that free mind, though an illuminating one, is a long path, and any individual undertaking Zen practice takes on a lifelong journey. It is a journey involving many techniques, and is similar to that of the painter as artist, as described by Lu Ch'ai.

Each chapter of this book begins with a Zen koan to provide examples of the nature of a koan. Nearby is a portion of the Heart Sutra, which is a classic sutra. In my view, the sutra provides a way to understand Eastern thought as well as providing fodder for meditation. In Buddhist practice, according to legend, the 100,000 verses of the sutras offer teachings on wisdom. All are based on the major themes of impermanence, non-self, nirvana, and the connection between nothingness and everything. They also reiterate the dictum to do no harm to any living thing, as we all are part of that seamless, living being.

> *The Heart Sutra*
>
> Form is no other than emptiness, Emptiness no other than form.
> Form is exactly emptiness, Emptiness exactly form.
> Sensation, thought impulse and consciousness are also like this.
> All things are marked by emptiness.
> Not Born, not destroyed.

The sutra may be of any length, although it most often is pithy and short, similar to the Heart Sutra, which is often chanted in meditation halls worldwide. The wholeness and integrity of the sutras, koans, and Zen meditation can be of interest to us as qualitative researchers if for no other reason than to help us understand ourselves and who we are in this universe.

Intuition, Creativity, and the Imagination

When I first wrote about intuition and creativity (Janesick, 2000), I used the metaphor of dance. In this book, I go further in the discussion, using the metaphor of Zen and of intuition, creativity, and the imagination. I see intuition, creativity, and an awakened imagination as the foundation of qualitative research as well as Zen. As Shakespeare put it:

The lunatic, the lover, and the poet
Are of imagination, all compact…
The poet's eye, in fine frenzy rolling
Doth glance from heaven to earth,
From earth to heaven:
And as imagination bodies forth
The forms of things unknown,
The poet's pen turns them into shapes and
Gives airy nothing
A local habitation and a name.

(A Midsummer Night's Dream, Act 5, Scene 1)

I have chosen to emphasize the importance of the imagination because it is hard to find that word in textbooks on qualitative research
or, indeed, on any kind of research. In Zen, practicing meditation involves tapping into your creativity. In his famous book on creativity,
Csikszentmihalyi (1996) describes a study of ninety-six creative artists,
scientists, inventors, and writers. The study was supported by the Spen-
cer Foundation over a four-year period. Csikszentmihalyi was curious
about intuition and creativity and about how and why creative people
do what they do. He described the creative process as having the following five steps (pp. 80-81):

> *Preparation:* Becoming immersed in something and arousing curiosity.
> *Incubation:* Ideas churn around in one's mind.
> *Insight:* This is the "aha" moment, the instant of realization.
> *Evaluation:* This is when the person decides if this idea makes sense
> or not, whether it is worth pursuing.
> *Elaboration:* This is the component that takes the most effort and time."

Csikszentmihalyi uses Edison's famous saying "Creativity consists
of 1 percent inspiration and 99 percent perspiration." There are many
epiphanies during this stage and all things change.

Csikszentmihalyi warns the reader not to take this description too
literally. Many of the writers and artists whom he interviewed mentioned how often they changed direction while realizing a big idea or
moment of curiosity. What struck me about the various testimonials in
the book was that nearly all the creative people mentioned a mentor,
teacher, or intellectual ancestor who inspired them in their creative ad-
venture. In meditation, as in qualitative research processes, we tap into
our creativity and we often work closely with a mentor. It is noteworthy
that the process of learning to meditate includes these same five steps
in the creative process.

Intuition is immediate apprehension. Intuition is a way of knowing
the world through insight and exercising one's imagination. I use the
term creativity in this book as having the quality and sense of creating
rather than of imitating someone or something. Meditation teachers
often say that meditation is a workout for our creative processes. It is
through intuition that we come to moments of realization about the
world, our communities, and ourselves. We also learn from those who

have gone before us, a point made by Csikszenmihalyi (1996) and the very point of Zen teachers. Those who have gone before us, our ancestors, play a critical role in the development of our creativity.

My first thought about intuition and creativity, when I read about Csikszenmihalyi's study, focused on initiating a conversation explaining the role of the qualitative researcher. Today, I understand that intuition and creativity are at the heart of qualitative work in terms of the design, data collection techniques, role of the researcher and possible co-researchers, and interpretation of any data set used in a study. I also think that creativity influences what we leave in and what we leave out of any given study. Similarly in meditation, we use creativity to leave in or leave out various thoughts and other content.

I consider intuition and creativity as the yin and yang of the imagination. In the study mentioned earlier, Csikszentmihalyi (1996) acquired many insights about creative individuals. Overall, he identified the following three ways to view creativity:

1. As in everyday, ordinary conversation, people who express stimulating, innovative, and unique thoughts are viewed as creative or even brilliant. Everyone should be encouraged to find ways to be creative in everyday life.

2. Individuals who experience the world are often referred to in unique ways. They are seen as the people who make important discoveries, and only they know of these discoveries. This viewpoint might be called personal creativity.

3. Individuals who have changed our culture in some unforgettable and critical way represent another category. To name a few examples, Leonardo Da Vinci, Thomas Edison, Martha Graham, Steve Jobs, Charles Dickens, Sylvia Plath, and Mark Zuckerberg all fit in this category. These individuals must make public an idea that shifts or changes our culture.

Creativity is a serious component of life. Many writers have pointed out that creativity is a human ability that separates us from the other living things on earth. Creativity often involves unplanned discoveries, and these discoveries often enrich our lives. For example, the astronomer Vera Rubin was part of the study of creativity. Here is her description of her unplanned discovery that stars belonging to a given galaxy do not rotate in the same direction:

It takes a lot of courage to be a research scientist.... You invest an enormous amount of yourself, your life, your time, and nothing may come of it. You could spend five years working on a problem and it could be wrong.... Discoveries are always nice. I just discovered something this spring that is enchanting. I remember how fun it was. (Csikszentmihalyi, 1996, p. 217)

Of course, Vera Rubin's description reflects a lifetime of hard work. She went on to speak of the persistent quality of creativity:

I had enormous doubts early in my career. It was nothing but one large doubt whether this would really work. It wasn't that I was unable to persevere. I was unable to stop! I just couldn't give it up. It was too important...but I was never really sure that it was going to work. (Csikszentmihalyi, 1996, p. 217)

Similarly, the poet Mark Strand developed ideas about his creativity and intuition and where they come from.

One of the amazing things about what I do is, you don't know when you're going to be hit by an idea. You don't know where it comes from. I think it has to do with language...it is a great mystery to me, but then so many things are.... I don't even know if my writing is a way of figuring it (life) out. I don't write to learn more about myself. I write because it amuses me.... I am always working.... Somewhere in the back of my head, I am writing, mulling over. (Csikszentmihalyi, 1996, p. 241)

It is curious that Strand mentions writing, as writing is indeed a form of inquiry. It is also a process of discovery, and this is well established in the literature. Richardson (2001) has argued that writing is a solid method of inquiry. She argues that writing should make a contribution to any given field or discipline and should have an aesthetic value as well. Further, the writing should be reflexive and should have an emotional impact and express some feature of reality. All this has to do with what Strand called "figuring things out." Further, both Rubin and Strand mentioned the unstoppable nature of their work. They felt that they could not stop. They also mentioned, as did others in the creativity study, that their work was satisfying and meaningful. The painter Ellen Lanyon added the following:

For a lot of my work…I worked with oil paint. Then in the early sixties, by chance, I started working with photographs. Next I went into the use of acrylics.… I spent five years training myself in the use of acrylics. So that now, most people don't even know they are not oil paintings.… In that process, I also changed the content.

That started in about 1968, and the work is still involved in that general area.… I mean it all sort of proliferated and moved along. (Csikszentmihalyi, 1996, p. 219)

Thus Lanyon shows still another facet of creativity, namely, that it is changeable, developmental, and autobiographical. There is also the notion of fulfillment related to the completion of a creative work, as seen here in the remarks of Robert Trachinger, a successful television producer.

I really want to enjoy life now. I want to kick back. I do some yoga. I do some Tai Chi. Teaching remains my great love…I am going to school. I am taking great books courses…I counsel young people. I am not a sage by any means but I've lived 67 years and there are some things I do sense and know. Caring is a good feeling, and we have lost our appetite for it. (Csikszentmihalyi, 1996, p. 224)

Each of the ideas about creativity documented here resonates, if not coincides, with the early work of John Dewey (1934) on the topic.

I have previously noted that artist and perceiver alike, begin with what I call a total seizure, an inclusive qualitative whole not yet articulated, not distinguished into members.… Moreover, not only does the "mood "come first, but it persists as the substratum after distinctions emerge; in fact they emerge as its distinctions. (p. 37)

Dewey uses the term intuition to refer to a pervasive sense of experience. He reminds us that art in any form is dynamic, holistic, and intuitive. The "seizure" is very like what we as qualitative researchers do when we are seized by the idea and design for a study. It is like the seizure of awareness of nirvana in meditation. What Dewey's work and Csikszentmihalyi's creativity study show us is the complexity of creativity and intuition and that at least three of the themes of pervasiveness, adjustability, and the autobiographical nature of creativity reiterate themselves. The creative act, the seizure of the moment of the creative act, and the autobiographical nature of the creative act are well realized. For qualitative researchers and for those who take a Zen approach, creativity may be nurtured and developed as we continue our work through the emphasis on the mind and thinking about, posing, and solving problems.

Creative people are constantly surprised and curious about the world. They find new ways to view and pose problems. They are not limited to their own field but are curious about many fields of study, and they read widely and look for the interconnections and layers of similarity in and among disciplines. Qualitative researchers and Zen thinkers, by definition, must be holistic, curious, and open to identifying problems, posing them, and finding creative solutions.

The thread of continuity appears in Csikszentmihalyi's creativity study as well. Threads from childhood and some early date are stamped onto the DNA of the creative person. Many spoke of following convoluted roads, yet always had a spark or curiosity about the current work in which they were engaged. For example, Linus Pauling always knew he would be a great scientist. Working in his father's drugstore, he was seized with the notion of working in chemistry. Similarly, Frank Offner, the famed electrical engineer and inventor, recalled,

> I know that I always wanted to play and make things like mechanical sets…. When I was 7 years old, we were in New York and I remember at The Museum of Natural History there was a seismograph and a stylus and…I asked my father how it worked and he said, "I don't know," and that was the first time…you know you think your father knows everything…so I was interested in how that worked and I figured it out. (Csikszentmihalyi, 1996, p. 99)

Offner went on to make many substantial discoveries. He developed transistorized measuring devices, the differential amplifier, and medical instrumentation. He figured out how to make the measurements in the electrocardiogram, the electroencephalogram, and the electromyogram. Again, what he and the other creative individuals demonstrate, and what we can learn from them, is a way to explain our work. We should be able to explain our creativity and intuition in terms of what we do. Zen meditation, itself a creative act, may assist us as well.

Zen Lessons

The ancient wisdom of the original and subsequent teachers of Zen philosophy and practice is only now being realized in the 21st century. This chapter begins with a brief outline of the generic history of meditation and its roots. The following historical timeline for meditation, which I learned about at the Chopra Center, gives us a greater appreciation of the power of meditation.

5000–3500	Archeologists and other scholars have found evidence and agree that meditation practices were rooted in certain cultures at this time.
1500 BCE	The Vedas of Ancient India (ancient Hindu teachings about living a spiritual life) testify to the strong presence of meditation.
600–500 BCE	Meditation takes hold in Taoist China and Buddhist India.
400–100 BCE	The yoga sutras, teachings of Pantajali, were compiled in this period. Meditation was outlined as part of yoga practice.
400 BCE–200 CE	The epic poem, the Bhagavad Gita, describing yoga, meditation, and spiritual awareness, was compiled. It was used as a guide to spiritual life in ancient times.
653 CE	The first meditation hall opens in Japan.
700–1700 CE	Translations in English and other western languages of the ancient teachings about meditation from India, China, and Japan appear in the West. Meditation is beginning to take hold, and today's growth can be traced to this period.
1920s–1950s	Translations continue, and major writers, artists, and poets continue to describe meditation, hatha yoga practice, and spiritual matters. Writers like Hesse and others, through fiction, nonfiction, and poetry, bring to light the possibilities in meditation. They wrote about seeing meditation as a way to health and well being.
1950s–1990s	Centers teaching meditation arise, such as the Mindfulness Stress Reduction Center at the University of Massachusetts in 1979 and the Chopra Center in 1996. Research designed to study the effects of meditation on health begins. Medical schools around the globe start to give credence to the value of meditation and to use it for stress reduction and healing. Many books and articles are published in this area by writers and scientists such as Deepak Chopra, Andrew Weil, Dean Ornish, and the great yoga writers and others (see Appendices A, B, and C for further information).

2000s–present   Growth in meditation practice and knowledge base is clear and documented. There is an increase in yoga classes, meditation classes, and awareness of meditation in books and articles, and information is available on WWW 2.0 applications for tablets and phones. Thousands of websites and other resources are available on the Internet (as is revealed by a Google search).

While this timeline is abbreviated, it emphasizes the historical nature of meditation and the strength of using Zen as a metaphor. Zen conjures up many words common to those who see the benefits of meditation. Because Zen emphasizes living in the present moment, the focus of meditation makes us give up worrying about the future and regrets about the past. This awareness alone can help qualitative researchers tremendously. For example, focusing on the *present moment* of the interview, without any clutter in the mind, can certainly improve the interview process. Likewise, there is no need to get upset or flustered if something unexpected happens to stop the flow of an interview. One of my doctoral students was upset when a phone call disrupted an interview with a school leader, but the call was about a potential bomb threat and the interview had to stop then and there. This situation exemplifies living in the present moment. It is Zen in action. You might ask how sitting in quiet and stillness for a length of time can be considered active. In fact, sitting zazen, that is, facing a blank wall, breathing, and repeating a mantra in your mind, is one of the most active things one can do. From science we learn that sitting still and focusing, in this case on a mantra or on just breathing and breath awareness, affects every cell in the body, blood pressure, and outlook on life. Surely this has resonance with our work with participants in the research projects that we choose to undertake. For qualitative researchers, paying attention to the moment is crucial to the stories that we eventually tell.

Meditation Lessons

The wisdom of the ancient teachers is present in the skeletal structure of meditation. Meditation teaches us to be still and to be mindful, rather than mindless, and is a way to keep the mind active. It also teaches us to breathe. Here is the connection between mind and body. All of these qualities can complement qualitative research techniques and structures. Zen, also known as mindfulness meditation, begins with breathing in and out. No matter what state of mind an individual is in at the moment of coming to the *zendo*, or meditation hall, or when meditating at home, the individual must come into the present moment. We who conduct qualitative interviews do this regularly. We must be attentive and be present, with our focus directed solely to the interview at that moment and in that space.

The following directions for beginning meditation can be useful for conducting a qualitative interview.

1. Sit in a quiet place, undisturbed, in a chair or on the floor with legs crossed, and listen to your breathing.
2. Breathe in and breathe out. If your mind goes somewhere else, bring it back to stillness.
3. Repeat this process. Continue to breathe in, breathe out, and relax.

Some meditation teachers recommend saying "Breathing in I am calm, breathing out I smile." A good way to keep track of meditation progress is to keep a meditation journal. By writing in the journal, just as a researcher might do when writing the reflective journal, the meditation student is able to follow his or her progress in the meditation process.

Another valuable approach to meditation is that of being still and counting from one to ten to calm and steady your mind. When your mind goes to a thought or idea, begin again, counting from one to ten. Counting helps to keep your attention on breathing and to clear a cluttered mind.

After some time using these two approaches, you may progress to what the transcendental meditation teachers and others recommend: the tried-and-true, mantra-based meditation. You must devote your *attention* to the meditation and must have the *intention* to keep to a steady course in your meditation practice. In my view, this approach provides a way for the qualitative researcher to be mindful and work toward mindfulness.

A well known tradition from the ancient practitioners of meditation is that of clearing the mind. We have lives full of distractions such as noise, media, and work trauma, yet we always hope to attain happiness. In the Zen tradition, happiness comes with silence, calm, and cleaning out the clutter. However, this state is the opposite of what society expects of us. Instead of rushing to meetings and conferences or from one activity to another, people practicing the Zen approach stop and do nothing. Most of us spend most of our time doing something. To stop and do nothing puts one on the Zen path, which is a path toward *emptiness* or *nothingness*. The state of emptiness is not a tragic unhappy state. Rather, emptiness helps one get to the core of non-self and, eventually, with much practice, to the state of nirvana, complete emptiness, and bliss.

The classic Zen approach to meditation is a meditation for clearing the mind. The following are typical instructions for this approach.

1. Sit quietly in a chair, or sit crossed leg on the floor or against a wall.
2. Pay attention to the first thought that comes into your mind.
3. Think about it for some time and then let it go.
4. Now try to sit with no thought.
5. When another thought comes, repeat this process.
6. Each time you repeat the process, notice that you are slowing down. In fact you might tell yourself to slow down. Some individuals use the words "slow down" as a mantra.

I consider these three basic approaches to learning meditation as the groundwork for understanding Zen. Just as there are multiple approaches to meditation, there are multiple genres and approaches to qualitative research. Over the past forty years, the literature on qualitative research methods has grown to include a multiplicity of well-documented books, journals, electronic journals, book chapters, handbooks, and articles. To name a few, possible methods for a qualitative research project are action research, ethnography, netnography, narrative research, historiography, case study, oral history, life history, biography, autoethnography, portraiture, fiction, and ethno-archeology.

Characteristics of Zen and Qualitative Research

Certain characteristics of the various approaches to qualitative research are much like the characteristics of Zen. Here are six shared characteristics for your consideration. First, both practices are holistic. Rather than piece or parse out data or meditation time, both attempt to understand the whole nature of things. In qualitative research, we try to understand and explain the social world as a whole. Using a Zen approach, we understand the whole of the whole. Second, both practices look at the relationships within a context. As mentioned earlier, with a Zen approach, there is a realization that we are all part of the whole, that we are connected to one another. In qualitative research, we study relationships because we are attempting to explain the whole. Third, both practices use the body and mind as key instruments. The literature relating to qualitative research frequently speaks about the researcher as the research instrument. The researcher has a body and mind. In Zen practice this duality is evident in the fact that, when sitting for meditation, the body must cooperate in order to allow the mind to free itself of clutter and simply exist. Fourth, both practices pay attention to the ethics of the social context and both agree that doing no harm is a given. Fifth, both practices rely on the power of storytelling. While Zen makes use of koans, sutras, and teachings in the form of narrative stories, qualitative researchers use storytelling as the major means of conveying the meaning of the research project. Sixth, both practices share a family of indicators, which include discipline in thinking and writing, persistence, diligence, intuition, and creativity. As a result of these similarities, Zen is a fitting metaphor for qualitative research.

Mindful Moment

When you begin to learn meditation there are many paths. You might consider breathing in and breathing out and simply saying the syllable "ho" as you breathe in and "hum" as you breathe out. Alternatively, you might use a mantra, selecting a word that is suitable as you progress. Saying the word "om" is a good way to start. Another reliable approach is counting from one to ten. As soon as you are distracted and your mind becomes muddled, start counting once again.

Contemplative Qualitative Inquiry

I use the term *contemplative inquiry* to refer to qualitative techniques that place a deep and serious emphasis on thought in every component of a study of the social world. From the first germ of an idea about a study, the design of the study is open to mindfulness. Throughout the actual conducting of the study, contemplative inquiry is solid in its awareness of the implications of impermanence, non-self, and nirvana, and it relies on intuition, creativity, and the imagination. The techniques of interviewing, observation, reflective journal writing, document and photograph review, and use of various media must all be practiced for a healthy time period. Finally, the aesthetic component of the research is a key element of the inquiry. Contemplative inquiry makes room for poetry, which can be used in multiple ways and at key stages in the inquiry. Just as Zen poetry is used widely before, during, and after the actual event of meditation, poetry can be used by qualitative researchers to portray the meaning of the literature review, the design, the data and the final story. Poetry is unlimited in its potential. Other aesthetic genres are welcome as well. For example, photography and its variations such as photovoice, painting, music, dance, digital storytelling, and the use of multimedia are also welcome in contemplative inquiry. It is not by accident that drums, flute music, cymbals, and bells are used during meditation. In this case, music calms the mind and the body. As Plato pointed out (taken from Grocke, 2006), "Music has the capacity to touch the innermost reaches of the soul, and music gives flight to the imagination." I view songs and music as another form of thinking.

Contemplative inquiry is also shaped by the questions posed in the inquiry. With a meditative approach to research, not all questions are suited to qualitative research methods. A review of the literature reveals that the following types of questions are suited to qualitative inquiry:

1. questions about the quality of a social system, a program, or an innovation,
2. questions about meaning and interpretation,
3. questions that are sociolinguistic, or language based,
4. questions about how things work,
5. questions about values and beliefs,
6. questions related to public policy,
7. questions that are viewed as controversial, and
8. questions in the postmodern world about race, social class, and gender.

This list is meant not to be extensive but to offer categories of questions suited to contemplative qualitative inquiry. Qualitative researchers are not tied to the notion of proving something. Instead, the intent of our work is to understand something. It is this research goal that drives the design of a qualitative research project. Working toward understanding is like Zen thinking. It is contemplation in action.

Summary

In this introductory chapter I have outlined some of the key elements of Zen to show how the metaphor of Zen is fitting and appropriate for widening our understanding of qualitative research methods. The most descriptive term for using this approach is contemplative qualitative inquiry. Key components such as impermanence, non-self, and nirvana were described, and basic terms from meditation practice and Buddhist vocabulary were introduced. Brief descriptions of approaches to meditation and of the contemplative approach to life and research were provided. Characteristics and types of questions common to contemplative qualitative research were presented.

Each of the nine chapters in this book includes a "Mindful Moment" to provoke thinking in new ways. They also contain "Mindful Activities" for practicing Zen and qualitative techniques. These features are included to provoke thinking, improve writing, and assist the reader in understanding qualitative methods in a new light. The Mindful Activities also have the following purposes.

1. To disrupt academic writing, which distances the reader and writer from each other and from the individuals involved in a research project. Academic writing further distances some readers in that a particular vocabulary, or jargon, is used in academia and many readers do not have access to that vocabulary. Thus, qualitative researchers write in ordinary language. In other words, we embrace subjectivity and prefer to focus on excellence in that arena.

2. To engage and educate readers of research. There are some who are not interested in qualitative research methodology. One of my goals for this book is to encourage people who think they dislike qualitative methods to take time to read about and think about qualitative methods.

3. To inspire readers of this book to push themselves further in understanding the use of metaphor, especially Zen, as a qualitative research metaphor.

4. To demystify the research process by writing as much as possible in ordinary understandable language. In this respect, contemplative approaches to qualitative inquiry can contribute to a more democratic research space. In other words, anything can be described and explained.

5. To democratize the research process, the writing up of research, and our understanding of research. Qualitative research techniques open up possibilities to many researchers in training who take responsibility for the rigor and high standards needed in practicing technique. Thus the ability to share research through the stories of participants connects and re-engages the reader and the writer of the report in the research process continuum.

6. To encourage readers to think historically; to familiarize themselves with the history of qualitative methods; and to read, think, and write about it if possible. To think about the long and elegant history of meditation practice, in this case Zen, is thinking historically. A regular component of studying Zen is to keep a journal of one's thoughts, thus contributing to the documentation of a person's history of his or her own mind.

How to Use this Book

I recommend reading this book from the front to the back. However, you may choose, after reading this first chapter, to go ahead and sample assorted chapters and to then go back and read from front to back. The goal should be to experience moments or sections of the text in a way that provokes new thoughts about a research project and new research activities. Using Zen as a metaphor, feel free to meditate on the concepts, ideas, mindful activities and on your own place in the contemplative research methods world. Experience is key to Zen practice and experience is key to qualitative research methodology. I hope you will experience this book as contemplative qualitative inquiry.

The Audience for this Book

By the nature of the topic, the audience for this book is anyone who appreciates qualitative research methods and is interested in learning more about using the metaphor of Zen practice in qualitative research.

This audience could include beginning, intermediate, and advanced qualitative researchers. It could include anyone who wants to learn something new about qualitative research techniques and processes. In my view, there should be no end to writing about observation, interviewing, research reflective journal writing, creating poetry, and applying meditative practices to research. When I first started writing about qualitative methods in the 1980s, I was writing for researchers in training and doctoral students, but it turned out that there were many audiences for descriptive writing about qualitative methods, including teacher educators and beginning teachers who wished to learn about interviewing and observing. Others interested were researchers in non government organizations (NGOs), health care professionals, and evaluation experts. Essentially, this book is for anyone intrigued by the topic.

Mindful Activities

1. Write a paragraph about one of your ancestors such as a grandparent or parent, aunt or uncle, or any family member who has influenced you in some way.

2. Write a few pages about your life, beginning with a moment that changed you in some way. Can you recall if any of your ancestors had something to do with this moment?

3. Begin working on a family history. Include in this history a timeline of your memories of key events in childhood, teenage years, early adult years, and the current stage of your life. Look for photos of yourself and of others who are influential in your life today. Start with a few ideas and develop them over a period of your choice, such as six months or a year.

Suggested Resources for Further Understanding

About Zen, Meditation, and Koans

Das, S. (1997). *Awakening the Buddha within*. New York: Broadway Books.
Das, S. (2000). *Awakening the Buddhist heart*. New York: Broadway Books.

Gach, G. (2004). *The complete idiot's guide to understanding Buddhism,* (2nd ed.). New York: Alpha Books.

Iyengar, B. K. S. (2005). *Light on life.* New York: Rodale.

Kabat-Zinn, J. (1994). *Wherever you go there you are.* New York: Hyperion.

Thondup, T. (2001). *Boundless healing: Meditation exercises to enlighten the mind and heal the body.* Boston: Shambala.

About the Theoretical Framework of Qualitative Research

Pascale, C. M. (2011). *Cartographies of knowledge: Exploring qualitative epistemologies.* Thousand Oaks, CA: Sage.

CHAPTER TWO

Impermanence and Observation

Kakua was the first Japanese to study Zen in China. Meditating constantly, he lived in a remote area of the mountain. Whenever people found him they asked him to say a few words, then he moved to an even more remote part of the mountain where he could not be found so easily. The emperor heard of this and asked him to come and say a few words. Kakua stood before the emperor in silence. He then produced his flute and blew one short note. Bowing politely, he disappeared.

One Note of Zen koan

Introduction

Thinking about impermanence is a beautiful thing. There are obvious connections to qualitative research methods. For example, all of the findings are tentative and changing. The very nature of qualitative work, as well as its strength, stems from the fact that whatever date we have fixed in time at any particular moment has a temporal quality. Someone else asking the same interview questions that you ask might find very different answers. Many considerations come into play, such as race, class, gender, values, time, and belief systems. The transcripts we work from, given to another person, might yield another set of findings and interpretation. Findings and recommendations on any given day might look very different six months later. At some point in life, as researchers in the social sciences, we all must come to the point of acknowledging that all findings are tentative. This understanding resonates with the notion of impermanence in Zen philosophy.

Valerie J. Janesick, "Impermanence and Observation" in *Contemplative Qualitative Inquiry: Practicing the Zen of Research*, pp. 41-51. © 2015 Left Coast Press, Inc. All rights reserved.

Impermanence can be confounding. Nevertheless, if we look to the natural world as Zen teachers often do, we see the fleeting nature of the seasons and the evolving life cycles in plants, animals, and human beings. There are lessons to be learned from the natural world that translate into the everyday work of the social scientist/qualitative researcher. From the Zen teachers, we learn that the notion of impermanence is humbling, for we see how tiny a speck we are in the cosmos. At the same time, it is the inspiration for meditation. Impermanence is the prompt for making our activities in this world a testimonial to doing no harm, whatever our life journey becomes. In order to do no harm, meditation leads us into a certain kind of awareness that is a *wide awakedness* to this world and to the people with whom we are connecting in work and home life. To be wide awake allows for understanding change and impermanence. All sentient beings are part of the boundaries of life and, as such, they all change. This notion is at the heart of understanding Zen and impermanence.

When I told someone I was writing about Zen and the art of qualitative research, he said something like, "That should be easy. You could just have 200 pages of blank pages." I was surprised at first, and thought that he intended the response to be humorous, yet it is actually quite profound. He was thinking of the notion of nothingness, emptiness, or just sitting in zazen meditation. As a result of the wisdom of early Zen teachers in having the learner seated facing a blank wall to avoid distractions, zazen meditation is powerful in its simplicity. It reiterates the fact that everything that I encounter is my life. Similarly, for qualitative researchers, everything that we encounter in our studies is very much a part of our lives. This notion is a Zen way of viewing the world of research. We think that we are what we write, yet our words are fleeting, or impermanent. They are the words I am writing at this moment, but when this book is finished, I will change and you will change. Again, we return to the heart of Zen, namely, that everything changes. Impermanence is the perfect way to characterize Zen. Likewise, meditation is the first step in freeing a person to change the habits that prevent insight.

Many famous writers have explored this idea in terms of their craft, even if they had heard nothing of Zen and impermanence. An example is the well known words of Jack Kerouac (1959) discussing essentials for writing prose. The following are some of his essentials that resonate for qualitative researchers and for Zen practice.

- Scribble secret notebooks, and wild typewritten pages, for your own joy.
- Be submissive to everything, open, listening.

- Be in love with your life.
- Something that you feel will find its own form.
- The jewel center of interest is the eye within the eye.
- Write in recollection and amazement for yourself.
- Work from pithy middle eye out, swimming in language sea.
- Accept loss forever.
- Believe in the holy contour of life.
- Struggle to sketch the flow that already exists intact in mind.
- Keep track of every day the date emblazoned in your morning.
- No fear or shame in the dignity of your experience, language, knowledge.
- Write for the world to read and see your exact pictures of it.
- Compose wild, undisciplined, pure, coming in from under, crazier the better.
- You're a genius all the time.

Kerouac was not the only writer to talk about the essence of writing. Stephen King (2000) wrote an entire book about this subject. I often use King's book *On Writing* in my classes. It resonates with students, especially the beginning writer, who has a beginner's mind. Zen teachers like to say that we all take a beginner's mind to heart. While King's book is a memoir about his approach to the craft of writing, he explores the themes of having a quiet place to write, writing every day, and being open to the world. His message to readers is to read a lot, think a lot, and write a lot, and to be aware of the dignity in their experience of the real world.

Observation and Impermanence

Since we are not talking here about impermanence as a metaphor, and since observation is one of our key techniques as qualitative researchers, how can we think about observation in this light? We observe to describe and explain a context, a physical space, and persons in a study. We observe the world around us. How is this impermanent? Does even the practice of observing a social setting teach us something about impermanence? I think about this question often as I teach qualitative research methods classes. I introduce students to the act of practicing observation through a series of developmental steps. We start by observing an object in still life, and we then observe people, then action, and finally a nonparticipant activity in a public space. This process is a warm up for the field work of a qualitative research project to be undertaken at some point in the future. I ask students to do the following as a practice exercise.

Nonparticipant Observation Assignment: A Public Space

Select a public space such as a coffee shop, shopping mall, book store, library, zoo, dog park, health club, funeral parlor, church, roller rink, nail salon, or movie theater.

Goal: To observe, describe, and explain that setting.

Action: Go to the place at least twice, or more often as needed, to get a sense of the complexity of the place. After you leave the field site, write about the meaning of the observation. Go on different days and at different times to see what changes occur, depending on the day and time. Take field notes to describe the setting, the people, and the action. If you take photographs, ask everyone photographed for permission to use the pictures. If you wish, draw a floor plan.

What to Look For:

The setting: Describe all components of the physical space as you defined and delimited it. For example someone describing a book store decided just to concentrate on the area of the café in the store and then on just two tables in the café and the counter. Another delimited the setting to the section containing the particular type of book she was interested in, namely, the cookbook.

The people: Describe the people in the space in a general manner and then describe one person in detail. What is the person doing? Concentrate your attention on this description. Some students have asked to take a photo, which helped later in preparing the narrative description in the final report.

The action: What is happening in the space? Are there groups of people? Describe what you see happening. Again, depending on the space, select a section of the area to describe. For example, a student who went to a shopping mall selected only the entrance to a dog boutique and observed the people going in and out and what they purchased.

Writing it up: When you leave the field, write up your raw notes, that is, the notes you took during your observations, and then rewrite them to create a narrative that describes the place, the people, and the action happening in that space. If you had all the time in the world, what would you like to know more about? What would you look for if you returned?

....

This assignment gets people attuned to, engaged in, and learning about a kind of observation that has a freedom to it, in that field notes are the recording device, possibly plus photographs and/or a floor plan. In the field of education, observation often is limited to returning to the classroom with a checklist. This kind of observation is not a checklist approach. Instead, it is training for free and open observation that provokes you to see what is before your eyes. This approach opens up many possibilities for the qualitative researcher in training. In terms of impermanence, if one were to return to that same space a few weeks or months later, it might be totally changed. The observations would be totally different, and the observer would also be totally different. Even observations of still life objects, animals, or people would change over time, as the person observing them changes over time. Zen meditation teachers emphasize impermanence through meditation prompts. Everything changes.

Observation Practices and Pitfalls

Learning about observation requires making many decisions before going into the field. The preceding, nonparticipant observation assignment has an outline and parameters, and field notes are required. It is an open ended assignment designed to get learners to see what is in the setting and see what is actually happening. The raw notes taken in the field have identifiers like date, time, place, and participants. I recommend leaving about one third of the space for Notes to Self. Here, the observer notes any idea or thought that is not part of the actual observation. For example, a Note to Self might be, "I need to return to find out if this happens regularly," or "I want to get a copy of the menu or price list to see what patrons are paying." Often observers write, "I need to return to get more details." The goal of observations in class and out of class is to describe in as much detail as possible various static and dynamic places, people, and events in the social world. To achieve this goal, I recommend that observation training start by observing something small and work up to observing something big. The following exercise exemplifies the order of observations that has worked for me (Janesick, 2011).

The Observation of Still Life with at Least Three Objects

The goal is to describe an arrangement of objects. This observation is done in twenty minute increments. After the first twenty minutes, class members read what they have written to each other and then repeat the exercise. I liken this process to preparing for the Olympics. As qualitative researchers in training, students need to develop sound habits for observation, interviewing, writing, and tapping into their creativity. By starting small with a few objects on a table, they are less intimidated by the process of observation. I often hear remarks like, "This is too hard" or "I can't do this yet." However, with a bit of patience and after seeing others writing, these objections usually fall away.

Observation of a Physical Setting

Next, again in twenty minute increments, the students observe and take field notes, share them with the group, and then repeat the process. This observation exercises the eyes to observe and actually see. Here again, students focus on one section of a space, for example, one side of a room, one set of picnic tables outside, or one table and two chairs at the Starbucks on campus. By warming up by observing a still life object, the student has developed a bit more confidence and is now getting the feel of the observation process, as well as learning how to focus in on one section of a given social space.

Observation of a Setting in the Home or Workplace

These observations follow the format just described. Bit by bit, step by step, just as in learning to meditate, the beginner starts to grow. To progress further, a person interested in practicing observation skills might easily continue by using the following progression.

— *Observation and Description of a Person You Know*
— *Observation and Description of a Stranger*
— *Observation of an Animal at Home, in a Zoo, or in a Pet Shop*
— *Observation and Description of your Favorite Vegetable*

....

I also use the provocative activity of drawing a famous artist's drawing upside down. In this case I use Picasso's well known drawing of Stravinsky upside down and ask students to observe it and draw it upside down. The goal is to view the drawing in a new light. This idea came from Betty Edwards (1999) in her book *Drawing on the Right Side of the Brain*. Most drawing books have similar exercises, and this one is remarkably helpful in training for observation. What is amazing about this activity is that students immediately utter objections like "I cannot draw." However, all seem to find a way to draw, and they themselves are completely surprised by the fact that they can indeed draw.

Many of my students are trained in the field of education and believe that observations have to do with the evaluation of a person in their work. Others think there is a set checklist which enables the student to sit in a classroom for a few minutes and simply check things off on a list. The students are amazed at the way in which we use observation in qualitative research projects, in particular by the focus required, the persistence, the need to return repeatedly to the site to get details, and the difficulty in capturing all of the detail in the raw field notes.

Moving developmentally from the observation of a still life object, to settings, to people, and then to a drawing, gives the student a strong appreciation for what is required in observation. Likewise in meditation, the student learns to train the mind and body in much the same way that a qualitative researcher learns to become a better observer. The act of observation helps students to remove themselves from the observation and become squarely focused on their description of the object, setting, or person. It is the enactment of non-self.

Observation sutra

We cannot create observers by saying "observe" but by giving them the power and the means for this observation and these means are procured through education of the senses.

Maria Montessori (2007)

Writing Up Observational Notes

After returning from the field, the next step is to read and reread the raw notes and then to write them up in a narrative format. Another set of decisions arises in the writing up process. Through what lens are you viewing these notes? Even before going into the field, it is a good idea to choose a theoretical framework to guide your work. In my field of education, most students find that their work fits with social constructionism or phenomenology. There are a great many theoretical frameworks ranging from obscure to self-evident; however, the two mentioned here, social constructionism and phenomenology, allow the observer to let the social setting, persons, and actions to be widely interpreted.

Details are crucial in the write up, but first, as a researcher, you need to decide on the style and type of narrative description. It is assumed you are following a preferred manual of style, and in our case we follow the 6th edition of the *Publication Manual of the American Psychological Association* (APA). Decisions relating to the write up include choosing a title for the piece that captures what you observed, achieving good flow throughout the piece, and, ultimately, drawing conclusions from what you observed. Finally, the write up should include a reflective piece on your skills as an observer. Keeping a journal of your reflections in the form of the researcher reflective journal is crucial, and recording in the journal your definition of your position (i.e., the theoretical frame for your study), your values, and your beliefs will make the process smoother later on in the final reporting of the study. Chapter 8 focuses on the processes and importance of the researcher reflective journal.

Ethics plays a role here as well. In the observation of activity in a public setting, researchers in training need to check with the person in charge of the setting and obtain their agreement for the research to be done there. Recently two students decided, unaware of each other's decision, to go to a Barnes and Noble café for the observation in different parts of Tampa. One manager welcomed the student, but the other manager refused, fearing his café would be evaluated. This incident illustrates the changeability and impermanence of the social world. It also allows for awareness of non-self, for the researcher realized, at the moment of the refusal, that nothing she could say would sway the manager to allow for nonparticipant observation on that day and at that time.

Eventually we are all involved in the art of telling a story, much like the Zen teachers. Practicing observation offers a way to become attuned to the context of the research project. Like the Olympian who trains body and mind, researchers train body and mind through seeing what is in front of them as they take notes and through writing up the narrative of those notes. When you move to doing research beyond observation, that is, to the qualitative interview, this warm up doing observation will help in identifying your role as a researcher.

The Observation and Writing Habit

As discussed earlier, the observation is only partly done with the raw notes and any further notes taken at the given site of the observation. The next step is to actually write a narrative description of the objects, the setting and context, any persons involved, and the action in the social setting. Through repeated observations, you develop the habit of observation and then writing. It is useful to keep your researcher reflective journal nearby so you continue reflecting in the journal. This process is similar to learning how to meditate. Practice both every day, and you will discover your meditation practice and your writing practice. In turn, this practicing will improve your observation ability.

Moon sutra

A Buddhist teacher was living in a simple hut far from any people. One evening he was walking and meditating. He returned to find a robber in his hut and so he said, "You have come a great distance to visit me. Here, take this shirt I am wearing as a gift." The robber was surprised and took the shirt and left. The teacher then sat down and meditated on the moon. "If only I could give the robber this stunning moon," he thought.

Summary

This chapter introduced observation, along with the idea of impermanence. Practicing observation developmentally is a good way to learn about becoming a good observer. Similar to meditation practice and keeping a meditation journal, practicing observation and keeping a researcher reflective journal will help you to become the writer you need to be so that your qualitative research reports engage your audience and make your reader care about the story you are telling.

> **Mindful Moment:** Imagine you are looking at a clear lake and your mind is like a clear lake. Think about its color and its shape. Then imagine throwing a pebble into the water. See the many layers of ripples in that water, the rippling effect and the quietude. Be still. Clear your mind of any clutter and try to reflect on the water. If your mind gets full of clutter, start again with the image of the lake, the ripples, and the quietude.

Mindful Activities

1. Write two pages about your early memories of your favorite hobby. How did you start this hobby? Learning to play the piano, figure skating, or scrapbooking, for example, might be good topics. Select the hobby, and write freely without any stops.

2. Write about a meaningful or recent vacation. Have you returned to that place? Were there any changes? Imagine what it would be like if you returned today. Make a list of places you might like to visit.

3. Write about your favorite teacher. What did you learn from that teacher? How has your life changed because of that teacher? Describe the teacher to the best of your ability.

4. Write two pages about your favorite fruit or vegetable and use a metaphor to describe the fruit or vegetable.

5. Seat yourself in any room in your living space and describe one section of that space.

Suggested Resources for Further Understanding

About Zen

Kabat-Zinn, J. (1994). *Wherever you go there you are: Mindfulness meditation in everyday life*. New York: Hyperion.

About Qualitative Research Methods

Keats, P. A. (2009). Multiple text analysis in narrative research: Visual, written, and spoken stories of experience. *Qualitative Research, 9,* 181-195.

Lawrence-Lightfoot, S. & Davis, J. (1997). *The art and science of portraiture*. San Francisco, CA: Jossey Bass.

Lichtmann, M. (2011). *Understanding and evaluating qualitative educational research*. Los Angeles, CA: Sage.

Lofland, J. & Lofland, L. (1995). *Analyzing social settings*. Belmont, CA: Wadsworth.

CHAPTER THREE

Non-Self
and Interviews

Unmon said, "I do not ask you about fifteen days ago. But what about fifteen days hence? Come, say a word about this!" Since none of the students answered, he answered for them. "Every day is a good day."

Every Day is a Good Day koan

Introduction

All qualitative researchers have to come to grips with the age old and primary techniques of observation, interviewing, and document analysis. By taking the Zen metaphor into this arena, particularly the non-self component, we can realize more clearly that interviewing, and more specifically, hearing the data from a participant, is a contemplative act. There are literally thousands of printed articles and hundreds of books on interviewing. Obviously, it has received a good deal of attention in the social sciences, arts, sciences, business, journalism, and society at large.

For the purposes of this book, we will look at interviewing in multiple ways. The first is by using the Zen metaphor to approach interviewing as non-self, that is, without the self interfering in the research. A second way is to approach interviewing as a creative act. And the third way is to use the storytelling nature of Zen through a koan or sutra to work toward a narrative approach and eventually tell a story. In our case, it is most often a written story. I have written earlier about interviewing as a habit of mind and a creative habit (Janesick, 2011). From that habit and moving towards understanding Zen as creativity, we can see another side of the verb "to interview" that includes the inner and outer aspects of interviewing. Many choreographers have written about the creative habit (Hawkins, 1992; Tharp, 2003; De Mille, 1991) and a number of social scientists, including Csikszentmihalyi (1996). In the field of education, it was John Dewey (1934) who wrote extensively on this topic. I mention these authors to point out the cross disciplinary nature of the idea of habits of the mind and body. A Zen approach to interviewing is an alternative way to approach interviewing both as a creative habit and as a contemplative act. In other words, interviewing may be considered an act of the imagination before it is put into action.

Arts based sutra

The arts inform as well as stimulate; they challenge as well as satisfy. Their location is not limited to galleries, concert halls, and theaters. Their home can be found wherever humans chose to have attentive and vital intercourse with life itself.

Elliot W. Eisner (1981)

Interviewing as a Creative Act

Thinking about the creative act of interviewing can a useful tool for qualitative researchers. Creativity is essentially about discovery, and interviewing allows for a great deal of discovery about a person's life and the social context of that life, as well as an understanding of ourselves as researchers. I use creativity here in the sense that Csikszentmihalyi (1996) views creativity, which is as a process by which a symbolic domain in the culture is changed. The act of interviewing is this kind of creative process, as the symbolic meaning of the interview, its analysis and interpretation, and its final narrative form change the landscape of the historical record. I think of it as insight interviewing. Each researcher, dancer, choreographer, writer, artist, or social scientist is called upon to develop habits of mind and body that change the culture.

All of the technical components need to be in order to facilitate the creative habit of interviewing. Practical habits to achieve this goal include checking the equipment for the interview ahead of time (e.g., testing the digital voice recorder), bringing an extra thumb drive for the recorder, and bringing a battery charger if the recorder is chargeable. In addition, being at the site of the interview ahead of time to test the equipment and see that the setting is in order is always a good practice. A good habit of mind, on the other hand, is to compose as many thoughtful questions as possible. It is far better to be over prepared than to get caught in an interview without questions. Developing these habits helps to make way for the creative act of interviewing.

Interviewing is probably the most rewarding component of any qualitative research project. It is a creative act that requires the use of imagination in much the same way that the choreographer imagines what the dance will look like. In addition to the habits previously noted, another useful habit is to read recent texts and articles on interviewing before the actual interview. For example, see Rubin & Rubin (2005) and Kvale (1996). I became interested in interviewing through social science texts, particularly oral history texts and feminist research methods texts that described interviewing in social constructionist terms, including those by Reinharz (1996) and Hesse-Biber and Leavy (2007). A good deal of what can be learned about interviewing may ultimately be learned by trial and error from long-term qualitative research projects. I defined interviewing earlier (Janesick, 2011) as a meeting of two persons to exchange information and ideas through questions and responses, resulting in communication and joint construction of meaning about a particular topic. With that definition in mind, as researchers in the process of conducting a study, we rely on different kinds of questions for eliciting various responses. A Zen approach to interviewing is similar to these approaches. This chapter revisits some of the processes of interviewing.

Interviewing and the Qualitative Researcher

Interviewing as a creative act of the imagination is one thing, but as the Zen teachers regularly mention, we all are rooted in our everyday activities and must attend to the details of those activities. There is a saying among meditation teachers that applies here, namely, "First, the laundry." In other words, we need to do our homework first. All the practical details must be in place before scaling the heights. Since interviewing is our mainstay technique oftentimes, we must pay attention mindfully to all that goes into the interview process. We rely on different kinds of questions for eliciting responses from various stakeholders. In two oral histories of female leaders (Janesick, 2004), I described various types of questions for qualitative researchers to think about when designing interviews. I am amending and extending those thoughts here, for study and reflection.

Types of Questions for Interviewing

In the field of qualitative research there is general agreement about the importance of interviewing, but many writers wish to push the boundaries of interviewing. Your practice and thinking will lead you to what works for your particular situation. The following examples describe the kinds of questions you might use in interviewing.

1. "Big umbrella" or "help me understand" questions
   - Can you talk to me about the recent decision you spoke of earlier which gave you such stress concerning putting students on probation?
   - Tell me what happened following this decision.
   - Help me understand what your typical challenges are like on a daily basis in your role as a teacher.
   - Help me understand your life as a parole officer.
   - Describe your day yesterday from the time you woke up till the end of the day.

2. Structural/paradigmatic questions
   - Given all the things you have told me about being a female superintendent, what keeps you going every day?
   - Walk me through a typical school board meeting.
   - What are some of your proudest achievements?
   - What are some critical incidents where you sought help in discussing the incident?
   - What decisions caused you to rethink a policy or procedure?

3. Follow up/clarifying questions
   - You mentioned that "face to face time with board members" is important to you. Can you tell me how you use this time?
   - Tell me more about what you mean about your description as a "techno guru" by the teachers you supervise.

— Can you explain your statement about "falling into this job"?

4. Experience/example questions

    — You mentioned that you are seeing students succeed in ways you never imagined. Can you give me an example of this success?

    — Can you give me an example of your most difficult day during your interviews for this position?

    — You mentioned that you laughed a lot. What keeps you laughing?

    — Can you describe a recent incident that got you laughing?

5. Comparison/contrast questions

    — You said there was a big difference between a great leader and an ordinary one. What are some of these differences? Can you describe a few for me?

    — You mentioned that there is no simple board meeting and at the same time you can almost predict what will be the point of contention at the meeting. Can you say more about this?

6. Closing questions

    — Is there anything you wish to add to our conversation today?

    — Is there anything I have forgotten to ask and you feel is important?

Closing an interview is often difficult for both interviewer and interviewee. A good rule of thumb for this situation is to ask questions that indicate the interview is ending and that enable the participant to keep thinking about the information already collected and, quite possibly, look forward to another interview. The preceding two questions are good for closing an interview. Many researchers report that participants will call a day or two later saying they are still thinking about the closing question and want to tell the researcher something that they forgot at the time of the interview. Anticipating this situation, the interviewer should always invite the person to email or call if they think of any additional information that is pertinent.

Preparing for Interviewing

Having questions prepared for your interviews is a good start, but you need then to adapt them according to the flow of the interview and feel free to probe further when something comes up that needs more elicitation. Also, it is often helpful to take field notes during an interview at the same as you are recording the interview on a digital recording device. Note taking and listening are both demanding activities, and it takes some time to feel comfortable doing them both at the same time. It is now possible to video and audio record on the same device. This approach provides a record of nonverbal communications, any movement or changes in the setting or place, or any other matters that come up.

As discussed earlier, a good rule of thumb for interviewing is to be prepared not just with your questions for the interview but also in terms of having all your interview equipment in good shape. The Zen saying "First, the laundry" means you should first take care of all the everyday details and tasks, so you can then concentrate on the meditation. Similarly, as a qualitative interviewer, you need to take care of the little details, the nuts and bolts, to ensure that your interview is as free from distractions and snags as possible. Being prepared, with a set of thoughtful questions, will make your job easier. It is far better to be over prepared than to get caught in an interview without questions. Five or six questions of the type just described are usually reasonable and may yield well over an hour of interview data on tape. The question "Tell me about your day as a former gang member" once yielded nearly three hours of interview data, that is, sixty pages of transcript data, leaving all the other questions for another interview time.

Now that you are prepared and practicing interviews, the next thing to be aware of is the massive amount of data yielded from your interviews. For each one hour of interviewing you can expect at least twenty pages of transcript. An important consideration, if you are having transcripts prepared by a professional transcriptionist, is the cost of transcriptions. Over time, you will develop a sense of awareness and timing about the participants in your study and learn how to rearrange things accordingly. Be sure to do a pilot study to test some of the questions you create. Find someone to interview and try out the questions. It will save you much time later on in follow up after the interview. It may also save in the cost of transcriptions.

Doing Interviewing and Transcriptions

This section discusses six strategies for successful interviewing and transcribing. First, be prepared, with materials such as your digital recorder and your notebook for field notes ready to go. Today, digital voice recorders are tremendously economical, efficient, and effective. For less than ninety dollars you can get a digital voice recorder with a thumb drive, which can then be attached to your computer and the interview put on a compact disc (CD). Also, if you are not doing your own transcriptions, the file can be sent electronically to a transcriber. Many of my students have either Olympus or Sony digital recorders and upgrade them every year. I myself have had four recorders over the past four years, each more sophisticated than the next. It is always a good idea to take at least two recorders to an interview to have a back up in the field, should one fail. Likewise, if your recorder uses batteries, take extra batteries.

Since most students currently seem to have iPads or iPhones, or similar devices, applications (apps) such as iTalk or iSpeak can replace the digital recorder. iSpeak, for example, converts voice to text and can store at least one hour of an interview. A little time spent researching this subject will enable you to find the best app for you. I use iSpeak at present, but with advances in technology, by the time this book goes to print I imagine something better will have come along. If you use any apps, be aware that they are updated or changed completely on a regular basis, so you should always have a backup plan ready in the event that your app fails.

Be sure and use technology to your advantage. Many of my students use digital video recording, which captures the participant's nonverbal cues as well as the spoken words. Digital video cameras are also readily available, and even secondhand sales on popular websites can provide working cameras. This approach provides both a visual and an audio history of a person's story, and is often useful at the point of member checking, that is, checking back with the study participants regarding the accuracy and content of the interview. Still another interview strategy is using Skype or FaceTime and then downloading the interview for transcription. This approach is especially useful when interviewing participants in other countries. Many of my international students regularly use Skype for interviews, which achieves a cost saving as well.

Second, before the interview, check to see that your recording device is functional. Test that your voice is being reproduced clearly on the tape by saying the date, time, and place and listing the participant/s. This practice is helpful later, not only when doing transcriptions but also for jogging your memory later on when you are ready to write up your narrative.

Third, give a copy of the interview questions to your participant ahead of time. This practice enables the participant to think about the questions ahead of time and thus may help to jog their memory as well as get to the heart of the information to be disclosed. You may even find that a participant will change the questions as needed, which is perfectly reasonable and part of the process in qualitative research. Also, remind the person of the interview time and place with a call and/or email. Checking in ahead of time is much more efficient than finding, at the last minute, that the person is unavailable for whatever reason and having to reschedule the interview. Remember, in field work anything can happen. Things change in a moment's time. It is to be expected that now and then people will cancel or forget an interview and have to reschedule it. In rare situations a participant may decide after an interview that this activity is not for them and drop out of your study. Be prepared with a backup list of participants for such a situation.

Fourth, remember the *categories of culture* that affect how you frame a question, deliver the question, take field notes as the tape is recording, and, ultimately, make sense of the data. Try not to assume that your participant thinks like you do or holds the same set of values or the same knowledge base. Such categories of culture include the following"

- *Cognitive culture*

  How do the interviewer and interviewee perceive their own context and culture? Although we all have some values and beliefs in common, it is a good rule to let the participant open up to you with their beliefs and values. We are alike yet not alike. Never assume that you and the participant understand each other completely. One of the checks and balances in qualitative work is that you continue the interview long enough to establish a connection with the interviewee and until you both trust one another, even if it means staying overtime. By using a series of interviews, you can build trust, leading to open communication and understanding.

- *Collective culture*

  How do both the interviewer and interviewee see themselves as part of a collective culture including gender, race, class, religion, and ethnicity? We are, each of us, unique and separate, even as we are members of a collective group. Again, be sure to spend time building trust and sharing information.

- *Descriptive culture*

  How do both interviewer and interviewee see all those written works and works of art and science in their respective worlds? One of the wonderful things about the arts and the sciences is that they inform and improve our lives. Recall that even at that, we all are informed in our own ways. Our lives are improved case by case. These have had an effect on both the interviewee and the person who takes the role of interviewer.

- *Linguistic culture or language*

  If you are interviewing in a language other than English, document who translated the interview. If you, as the interviewer, transcribed the interview and translated it, explain that process and your experience with the other language.

Fifth, remember that one often makes assumptions while interviewing someone and often falls into old habits. Be aware of the following situations.

- *Assumption of similarities*

  If, for example, you act professionally in the role of an educator and are interviewing another educator, do not assume a similarity of thoughts, beliefs, and values. In Zen thinking, we are all one in the universe and our true self is realized in meditation. By coming to know your place in the universe you can learn to see the similarities and differences between and among interviewer and interviewees.

- *Language difference*

  The importance of one's first language and the misinterpretation of meaning in another language can be critical. In St. Exupery's classic *The Little Prince* (1943), he mentions that "words are the source of misunderstanding." In our work as qualitative researchers we work toward using words for understanding rather than interfering with understanding. In cases where the interviewing is conducted in a language other than English, be clear in your explanation of how the interview was transcribed, who transcribed it, and list the qualifications of the transcriber.

- *Nonverbal misinterpretation*

  Obviously we may all read nonverbal language incorrectly, which is why you should interview someone more than once and keep coming back to find answers to your questions. The wisdom of staying in the field and the setting for as long as is needed comes into play here.

- *Stereotypes*

  Before beginning an interview, check yourself for any stereotypes you may hold and be clear about them in your description of your role as a researcher. Writing about this subject in your reflective journal may also be useful, and could well be part of the eventual description of your role in the research project.

- *Tendency to evaluate*

  Some educators continue to evaluate every spoken or written word, even outside the classroom. Try to avoid evaluating the content of the participant's remarks. Practicing Zen breathing and staying calm will help you to follow the Zen dictum of "no judgment."

- *Stress of interviewing*

  If you are feeling stressed, the person being interviewed may sense your state of mind and allow it to affect their responses. Go to the interview prepared, use all your active listening skills, relax, and enjoy the interview. Put aside any road blocks obstructing your ability to hear data. Breathe, be calm, and hear the data.

Sixth, construct clear, open ended questions, and then allow the person to respond. Avoid interrupting participants in the study. Also, avoid asking leading questions or making leading remarks. Silence is a beautiful thing. Be patient and let the participant think. Be calm. Listen and hear the data.

Individuals who are new to interviewing often find it hard to allow the participant/narrator to speak without interruption. Some researchers in training find silence uncomfortable. There is no need to fear silence. In fact, silence may help to produce some amazing information. Here are some rules of thumb that a group of us discussing this topic recently prepared. We think of them as a laundry list.

- *Be aware of time.* Stop when you promised to stop, rather than letting an interview go on and on. Do not be afraid to make an appointment for another time. Recall that the participants are giving you precious time in their often-filled schedule.

- *Let there be silence once in a while.* If there is a lull in the interview, be aware that the person may be thinking ahead or recalling something. Silence is often a sign that the participant is truly grappling with your questions.

- *Ask for any papers, documents, photos, or artifacts that have been mentioned in the interview.* These materials may be used later when you are writing up your narrative. For example, ask for a resume or curriculum vitae, a course syllabus, or any other document that may help you make sense of the participant's world.

- *Leave the door open for future contact.* Ask if you may return, email, or call. Ask what is the best time to call. Invite the participant to email you as well.

- *Always follow common courtesy and ethical principles and always thank the interviewee.* If you are working online with a participant, for example, a Skype interview, follow standard Netiquette as well. Netiquette is etiquette on the World Wide Web. As for thanking your participants, in some cases researchers offer to take the person out for coffee or lunch. How to say thank you is an individual preference, but some sort of thank you does make the interview situation more humane and may help to establish rapport, trust, and continued communication. Some researchers, on completion of a study, give a small gift to their participants such as a gift card, a book, or some meaningful sign of appreciation.

- *Feel free to find a mutually agreeable balance, where professional relationships between the interviewee and interviewer have already been established.* In terms of ethical considerations, it goes without saying that it would be wrong to interview someone where a relationship exists that puts the interviewer in the role of evaluator or employer. The interviewer should never be in a dominant role where information could be extorted or misused. Last, written consent from the particpants must be obtained before the interviews are conducted.

With awareness of some of the techniques of interviewing as well as the potential ethical issues involved with interviewing, you are ready for the demanding task of analyzing interview data and making sense of it. Thinking about and contemplating the interview and the transcript is a key part of the process, and writing about the process in the researcher reflective journal will help. A good rule on completing an interview is to transcribe it as soon as possible. Many transcription services are available on the Web, in the event that you are unable to do your own transcriptions. Production Transcripts in Los Angeles, for example, is one of the most active (see www.productiontranscripts .com). Another, CastingWords (see www.castingwords.com), is considered effective and efficient in terms of turnaround time and content. By having the transcripts in hand, the researcher may read and reread them in the process of analysis and interpretation. Researchers look for major themes, key words, and indices of behavior and belief and make an initial list of major and minor categories. Every attempt is made to look for critical incidents, points of tension and conflict, and contradictions to help in interpreting the data.

Summary

This chapter discussed interviewing as a creative act, preparing for the interview, constructing questions, journal writing to augment interviews, and ways for the qualitative researcher to look at data. Interviewing is the mainstay of our work as qualitative researchers. It can be seen as a creative contemplative act dependent on developing good habits of mind. The following are good habits to develop as a researcher in training.

1. Be prepared with technology. Before going out into the field, check that you have all your gear, test it all, and be sure it is functioning to your satisfaction.
2. Be prepared in terms of content of the interview. Know your questions inside and out.
3. Be prepared with some practice interviewing or a pilot study to test out your questions.
4. Be prepared to encounter problems in the social world. The interviewer shows up for the appointed interview and the participant has been called away on an emergency. What do you do?
5. Be prepared to read a great deal. Read everything you can find that relates to the person you are interviewing.
6. Be prepared to listen to what is being said.
7. Be prepared for the unexpected. Since the social world is always active, rather than static, be prepared for everything that the chaos of the social world can bring. The Zen approach is that everything changes.
8. Be prepared to use the arts. Using poetry, photography, or other artistic forms can only enhance your final reporting.

9. Use documents as needed to augment the final narrative. Interviews and observations carry a great deal of power and can be enhanced with documents such as a data set.

10. Keep a researcher reflective journal. This practice is a life saver for any thoughtful researcher.

11. Find the theoretical frame that guides your research as early as possible when designing your study.

12. Tune into your IRB. You will need IRB approval to do your interviews. This point will be taken up more fully in the following chapter.

Mindful moment: Not doing anything. Sit in your meditation area and let your body relax. Or, lie down on your yoga mat and let your body calm down and relax. Don't do anything in particular. As you become accustomed to doing nothing, you will relax more fully. Be calm and relax. Be patient with yourself. Allow this to happen. After this, write about this experience in your journal.

Mindful Activities

1. Write three pages to yourself in your journal in dialogue format, writing about what you want to learn from your project.

2. Write three pages about the culture in which your interviews are taking place.

3. Write three pages about the high school experience that defined who you are today.

Suggested Resources for Further Understanding

About Qualitative Research

Kvale, S. (1996). *InterViews: An introduction to qualitative research interviewing.* Thousand Oaks, CA: Sage.

Leavy, P. (2012). Transdisciplinarity and training the next generation of researchers: Problem centered approaches to research and problem based learning. *International Review of Qualitative Research, 5*(2), 205-223.

Reinharz, S. (1992). *Feminist methods in social research.* New York: Oxford University Press.

Rubin, H. J. & Rubin, I. S. (2012). *Qualitative interviewing: The art of hearing data,* (3rd ed.). Thousand Oaks, CA: Sage.

Wolcott, H. (2009). *Writing up qualitative research,* (3rd ed.). Los Angeles, CA: Sage.

CHAPTER FOUR

Interviewing as an Act of Compassion: Do No Harm

Joshu began the study of Zen when he was sixty years old and continued until he was eighty, when he realized Zen. He taught from the age of eighty until he was one hundred and twenty. A student once asked him, "If I haven't anything in my mind, what shall I do?" Joshu replied, "Throw it out." "But if I haven't anything, how can I throw it out?" continued the questioner. "Well," said Joshu, "then carry it out."

Joshu's Zen koan

Ethics in Research and the Institutional Review Board

All qualitative interviewers face perennial ethical issues as they move from the interview to the writing up of the narrative. Those of us who work in the field of education have additional requirements. We have greater sensitivity to this notion because we work in a public arena and have to answer to many publics. Federal and state regulations and rules of accrediting bodies and Institutional Review Boards (IRBs) influence our work. As a result, we simply accept the fact that we will always be dealing with ethical issues at all phases of our research. All researchers work with IRBs, but because of the composition of IRBs and other factors, qualitative researchers are often more constrained. Some of the basic and perennial ethical issues concern confidentiality, anonymity, and, in this high-technology era, the documentation of everyday life.

Valerie J. Janesick, "Interviewing as an Act of Compassion: Do No Harm" in *Contemplative Qualitative Inquiry: Practicing the Zen of Research*, pp. 67-80. © 2015 Left Coast Press, Inc. All rights reserved.

What is one to do? I like to err on the side of caution and follow the rule "Do no harm," a caveat of Zen that fits nicely with the work of qualitative researchers. In fact, the concepts of respect, beneficence, and justice complete the notion of doing no harm. Beneficence is defined as doing kindness, and is a perfect connection to the loving kindness and compassion of Zen. Later in this chapter I recount five recent examples of qualitative researchers working with the IRB and tackling some of these issues.

In terms of confidentiality and anonymity, using the actual name of the participant has become an issue. On the one hand, when you document a portion of a life, you want the reader to know whose life it is. On the other hand, regulatory bodies, and in certain situations the participants themselves, often ask that names be changed in the process of the member checking of data or the writing up stage of the final report. The IRB at my institution requires verification of a name change by a written statement from the participant.

If a participant wants a name change to ensure some modicum of safety or for any other reason, I always agree to the change and ask the participant to come up with the new name. Many of my graduate students have been refused IRB approval because they wished to keep the actual names of the participants in a given study. This, by the way, was at the request of the participants, who insisted that their names be known. A good middle course of action that my students agreed to is to use the letters of the person's actual name to create a pseudonym. For example, the name Elizabeth Cunningham could be reformulated as Beth Chung, thus using the letters from the original name and, at the same time, appeasing IRB members who object to actual names. While this is not a perfect solution, it can be viewed as a good compromise.

Another useful strategy is to use symbolic names. If the person's new name suggests the meaning of the person's life, it helps in understanding the narrative. A student who recently studied outstanding female principals chose to name the participants as famous historical female leaders such as Eleanor Roosevelt, Hillary Clinton, Sojourner Truth, and Margaret Thatcher to suggest the qualities of each participant. Each of these names captured the data and themes of the study. Ongoing ethical issues require attention in all qualitative research projects, as well as ethical issues that may arise in each particular study. If and when additional issues arise, they should be worked out with the participant and explained in your final report.

The IRB recently created new demands for projects in oral history, action research, autoethnography, life history and some types of action research. The most trying is the insistence on changing the names of the participants in research studies. One wonders if it is possible to have complete anonymity in our technological world, which is designed to avoid privacy even when pseudonyms are used. Nonetheless, we can only do our best to safeguard participants and still stay true to the purposes and vision of the study. As universities become more corporate, the IRB also becomes more corporate. As Howard (2006) points out, some professors are reluctant to have their students interview Grandma! It will be enlightening to see what evolves next in terms of IRBs and our work with human participants. We are at the beginning of an era when social scientists will have to make the effort to educate IRB members when issues come to the fore. It is in our best interest to do so. If we do not educate them, who will?

Take for instance the issue of using blogging in a qualitative research project when the blog is private and only between the researcher and the participant. In a recent instance, a graduate student proposed to use blogging as one of several data collection techniques in her study. The IRB refused approval because of the blogging. After written communications, phone calls, and face to face meetings, it was ascertained that the IRB reviewers thought that blogging would result in a lack of confidentiality and anonymity. They thought blogging was open to the entire population on the World Wide Web. The researcher then explained how one could arrange for a blog to be private and confidential and that the actual name of the person would, of course, be changed. The entire saga took over six weeks and was a bit exhausting. As a result, the researcher decided to write about this experience to alert up-and-coming researchers and suggest that they go overboard in terms of explanation and specificity when communicating with the IRB about how a blog can be used effectively in qualitative projects.

Lessons Learned as a Former IRB Member

Something of a controversy has been brewing in academia since the 1990s about the need for IRB approval in certain interviewing projects or in oral histories, life histories, biographies, action research projects, and autoethnographies. It seems that some IRBs disavow these approaches and, in fact, say that the IRB approval is not needed since they are not actually research. To me this signifies a misunderstanding of these approaches. On the one hand, we want to protect participants by getting IRB approval for all research projects but, on the other hand, the federal regulations indicate that IRB approval is not needed, for example, for oral history projects, basically because oral history is not scientific in terms of generalizability and hypothesis testing. I mention this example to illustrate the solid adherence to post-positivist and "scientific" doctrine. In 2004, federal guidelines exempted oral history from the IRB process. Universities responded in various ways. Some said, "Fine. We are done with the IRB on any interview projects." Others said, "This is nonsense. Interviewing of any kind is research, including life history, oral history, biography, and some action research projects of a qualitative nature." Since then, things have been changing, depending on which university becomes involved in these cases. Over time, I have become increasingly interested in the problems arising for qualitative researchers, particularly doctoral students using alternative approaches to research. As a qualitative researcher all my professional life, an oral historian in the past two decades, and a recent member of the IRB at an institution where I worked previously, I am able to look back on the lessons that I learned from these experiences.

I was an active IRB member for a three year term and was the only oral historian, let alone qualitative researcher, of eleven members. The university was in a metropolitan area and had a student population of around 7000 students. At the time, there were only two kinds of doctorates offered at the university, the Doctor of Education (Ed.D.) and the Doctor of Psychology (Psy.D.). The work load was steady, and there was one IRB. In contrast, at my current institution, there are 36,000 students and six IRBs, five IRBs for medical research studies and one for all others, which are mostly in the social sciences and humanities. At the time of my service on the board, I was coincidentally the program director of the doctoral program in the College of Education. My students were directly affected on a daily basis. The types of questions asked of qualitative researchers by IRB members, the ethical issues raised by these questions, and the burden put on the shoulders of the researchers have raised my interest to the point of writing about the subject. In this section I describe five instances in the experience of my students that illuminate possible strategies for dealing with the IRB.

Mindful Moment: Never give up. No matter what is going on. Develop the heart. Be compassionate. Work for peace. Never give up.
Tensin Gyatso, the XIV Dalai Lama

The title of these examples could be "the researcher and participant relationship and the thorny issues of journal writing, technology, blogging, and confidentiality." The examples draw on the experience of individual graduate students who were studying practitioners in public and private schools as well as community venues. The students were interviewing participants for life histories, observing them, and keeping a researcher reflective journal. They also asked the participants to write reflective journals, and they asked for site documents and any artifacts that the participants might think were valuable for the study. In addition, one doctoral student did an interactive journal with the participants, and some researchers used private confidential blogging between themselves and individual participants. In recording these techniques on the IRB form, the researcher students were direct, descriptive, and forthright. Unfortunately, all applications were returned with similar questions, preventing the students from moving on in their research for periods of one to six months or, in one case, even longer. One of the goals of the IRB was to "meet regularly" and achieve a "timely turnaround," with its decision to enable students to proceed with their work. Nevertheless, the questions and comments returned to the prospective researchers came with few suggestions or alternatives, even though the students replied deftly and purposefully.

All the students were female professionals with many years of experience in educational leadership at all levels of work, elementary school through university. They were persistent with emails and phone calls to IRB members and face to face meetings with them. These examples are summaries of the more lengthy dialogues that took place. They are related here to serve as learning examples for prospective qualitative researchers as they begin to deal with IRBs. In each case, approval of the project was held up until the researcher responded in writing and resubmitted the form a second or third time. This process was astounding to the students, who had engaged with the IRB in good faith, produced all the correct forms, and wanted to proceed with their research projects.

IRB member: "Why keep a journal? These are too personal."

Researcher's response: The researcher presented the IRB member with a three page bibliography on the books, articles, and book chapters on this topic. The argument presented was that the history of journal writing in the arts and sciences goes back in time for centuries. In this case the researcher used a historical argument to win over the IRB member. In addition, the researcher argued that the confidentiality and anonymity agreement signed by all persons involved in this project protected all of us, including the university. The researcher strengthened her argument by citing a legal case which supported her position. Hearing these responses, the IRB member then voted to approve the project. Recall that if even one IRB member raises questions, the entire process may be stalled.

IRB member: "Who is going to read these journals?"

Researcher's response: "Please go to Page X where it states that only this researcher and these participants will read these journals." Having discussed the topic with the IRB member by phone before the face to face meeting, the researcher had brought written evidence to the meeting to remind the IRB member that this fact was clearly stated in the proposal. Eventually, in order to get her proposal approved, the researcher agreed to use one example from the reflective journal that related only to her own recollections of her research process and to place it in the appendices of her dissertation. She believed that this was the only option for her to gain approval at the time and she wanted to move on and finish the project.

IRB member: "How can you have a co-researcher in a project?"

Researcher's response: "While it is surely possible that in your field you may not have imagined this or used it, let me tell you that our field of educational leadership has been doing this for some time. Here is a bibliography to help you understand this growing body of literature." In addition, the researcher was savvy enough to know that she had to find an example of this approach in the field of this IRB member, a psychologist, and she found one rather effortlessly. She inquired into the names of current doctoral students in psychology and found three examples in recent dissertations in that department. Nonetheless, the IRB member then requested of the applicant that she provide an article, book, and other supportive evidence before he would sign off on her project. She provided the evidence and he approved the project.

IRB member: "It is unethical to observe people."

Researcher's response: "Perhaps you have forgotten the long and elegant history of observation, description, and explanation, which is the cornerstone of all good science and research. In fact, here is an example of the definitions from various dictionaries about the word 'empirical,' which translates to direct observation of experience and the real world experience. I will be happy to show you the *Handbook of Qualitative Research*, 2nd ed. (Denzin and Lincoln, 2000), which also has many fine chapters related to this topic. I also brought this five page annotated bibliography which details for you some books on qualitative research methods, along with some sample illustrative studies that successfully incorporate observations and interviews, like my proposed study. Feel free to keep this copy for your own library."

One IRB member was trained in psychology and was particularly disturbed by the word "harm" in the consent form. (Note, by the way, that the word "harm" is used in the federal guidelines). Nonetheless the researcher changed the phrase to accommodate the member's request. She also argued that the federal guidelines, when referring to harm in a research project, are taken in a global sense, that is, the amount of or chance of harm coming to a person in any given day of normal everyday activities.

IRB member: "How do you know you are not harming by keeping these journals on line, and blogging? Blogging is open to far too many people."

Researcher response: Here the IRB member allowed the consent form with the words "no harm will come to me." However, the member was concerned about interviewing as a research technique. The doctoral student responded saying, "As you can see, my questions provided in the application interview protocol are designed to gain information about a female school leader's views on her work. Let's take a look at these questions and as we do so, can you tell me which you think are harmful?

- Describe for me your typical day as the leader of this school.
- Can you talk to me about your single most noteworthy achievement?
- Can you think back over this past year and describe a situation which caused you to seek outside help on any matter?

- Can you talk about a situation where you struggled and struggled over a solution to a problem at the time, yet now months later, can only laugh about it?

- I can assure you that I am asking these questions of a remarkably sophisticated and articulate professional to help me to achieve the goals of my study. In no way are these intended to be harmful in any way."

Some researchers were using electronic journals from time to time. Many used the site www.penzu.com, which is fully protected, confidential, and accessed with a password. Thus, the entire world cannot drop in and view what is written. I encourage anyone who uses the Penzu site to write about the advantages of journaling using the Web. They also apply to journaling using private, confidential blogs.

The preceding five examples illustrate the numerous questions posed to qualitative researchers by IRB members. In the process of responding to the questions, the following became clear to the students.

1. Some IRB members had skimpy knowledge of the theory, history, and work of qualitative researchers in general and, in fact, regularly stated they were not interested in these matters. This conclusion awakened me to the realization that we need to educate IRB members about our research techniques. As a result I suggest that we all try to explain each situation as fully as possible as questions arise. Interestingly, by establishing a working relationship with the IRB office staff, I found a way to get things facilitated.

2. Some IRB members were imposing a standard for qualitative researchers unlike that of other researchers, for example, requesting additional statements that were not required by the federal guidelines and not required of those using quantitative methods.

3. Some IRB members had never actually thought about including qualitative researchers on the IRB. The only reason I became a member of the IRB was that I raised the issue of the questioning of qualitative researchers being disproportionate compared to that of the applicant pool with the Provost of my institution. The Provost, who appoints members to the IRB said to me, "You are now a member of the IRB effective immediately."

Every instance of students having proposals refused and sent back for further updates touched on the ethical issues of confidentiality, anonymity, and technology usage. As qualitative researchers we need to adopt strategies to actively address the following questions:

- How can qualitative researchers be proactive in foreseeing and addressing the eventual questions asked by IRB members who may not know the history, practice, and literature of our field?
- How can we be proactive and gain IRB membership?
- How can we do a better job in explaining what we do?
- How can we learn the culture of the IRB at our institution?
- How can we keep better track of the time required for qualitative research projects to gain approval?

As illustrated in the five examples, the types of questions sent back to the prospective researchers were revealing. In many instances they showed a surprising absence of understanding the nature of observation, interviewing, and journal writing. Particularly surprising was the resistance to interviewing, journal writing, or any technique that focused on *personal meaning,* on the clearly stated grounds that too much personal information would be forthcoming. Luckily all of the students were persistent in responding to the questions and cited supporting evidence from a current research methodology text. Their persistence was not just in written form, though that was powerful. The students also made numerous phone calls, sent numerous emails, and tried to track down the IRB member to speak on behalf of their application. Essentially, they became activists advocating for their research. As a sort of soothing balm, many of the students wrote about this experience in their dissertations or in subsequent written work on the topic of ethical issues and fieldwork. Others just changed the description of their method to a generic case study, which seemed to have worked in terms of gaining IRB approval, even when they used the original techniques. These researchers in training, who are going on to be the next generation of researchers and professors, swore that they would be extremely vigilant in the future in terms of their own students' interactions with IRB members. All of this leads back to the core issues of confidentiality, anonymity, and the use of technology and to the guiding rule in a Zen approach, which is to do no harm.

Given the behavior that student researchers experience at the hands of the IRB in some cases, there is reason to be concerned. The implications of this situation are many. First, findings from qualitative research projects will be heard less often in policy forums, if at all. At the same time, we know that individual case studies yield a great deal of data that can be used by other researchers, and findings from this source could very well influence policy. Second, qualitative researchers need to assert themselves and challenge traditional, elitist approaches to research. Third, future researchers who use qualitative research methods will need to be equipped to deal with IRBs in the event they are put upon to answer extra questions that delay the approval process.

Qualitative researchers need a space to talk through this state of affairs. Professional meetings provide one way to raise the level of interest and discourse on these matters. Another is that of writing. Notable journals in various fields are dedicating entire journals to these topics of ethical issues and the IRB. For example, nearly an entire issue of the journal *Qualitative Inquiry* (Vol. 10(2), April 2004) was devoted to substantive questions and issues related to IRBs and qualitative research.

Approaching IRBs as an Innovation

The recent literature on innovations suggests that innovations can succeed when all parties involved learn the language at hand, get on board, develop an open mind about the innovation, and gain membership in the process itself. While qualitative research has an ancient and firm pedigree and, in fact, is older than statistical methods, recasting our work as an innovation might help to persuade traditional elites about the meaning, value, and power of qualitative research projects. I have always found it helpful to stress the long and eloquent history of qualitative research and back that up with a list of references and resources.

The famous *Belmont Report* (1978) contains the code eventually adopted for research guidelines for the IRB regarding research using human subjects. The three ethical principles set forth in the *Belmont Report* are respect for persons, beneficence, and justice. They are meant for the protection of participants in a study. However, they work both ways. I see them as respect for researchers, and for beneficence and justice for researchers. Respect for persons includes supporting human dignity and obtaining informed consent, beneficence involves protecting them from harm and minimizing the risks in research, and justice requires that the benefits and burdens are distributed fairly. These goals resonant with the Zen principles of compassion and loving kindness and the idea that we should do no harm to any living thing. The report defined research in terms of hypothesis testing and the generalizability the result. Obviously this definition has the potential of creating problems for any forms of qualitative research. I found that many IRB members were swayed somewhat by references to material on the World Wide Web. In that spirit, it is always a good idea to educate the IRB members as needed.

All in all, the Web is a good source for up-to-the-minute ethics discussions, blogs, policy changes, and guidelines that may be of assistance to researchers. Other resources are journals, most often in education, the humanities, medicine, pharmacy, and social work. In particular, the journal *IRB: Ethics & Human Research* is an outstanding resource. In reviewing many of the websites, I identified a cluster of issues that include but are not limited to the following and that merit further study.

1. Studying children, interviewing them, or even just observing them raises questions of an ethical nature. Some of these questions revolve around issues of informed consent, ability to answer questions without fear of judgment or dislike, and issues of children's rights.

2. The subject of anonymity raises the question "How anonymous is anonymous?" For example, from the usual description of persons, places, events, and from the location of the university where the dissertation is being completed, can it be that difficult to identify which institution, which persons, and which sites are being studied? Today many individuals have a mobile phone or other recording device with them at all times. We may all be in someone's movie at some time or other.

3. The issue of confidentiality is related to the techniques of journal writing either on the Web at a private site such as Penzu or in a journal written by hand with pen and paper.

4. We need to come to grips with the ubiquitous use of technology. We have a generation of digital natives who blog, use social media, and are comfortable with a digital world. How can we use this effectively?

What have I learned as a former member of the IRB? Among other things, I have learned that consideration of ethics has been reduced to the area of informed consent, and that informed consent is simply a matter of stating that no harm will come to anyone other than the harm of ordinary living. In addition, I believe that the IRB institutional forms are designed to avoid legal action. The form itself is born of the perspective of a modernist medical model, and qualitative research projects often are postmodern, if not beyond the postmodern era. Qualitative researchers need to learn how to describe their proposed projects in the modernist idiom without sacrificing the story and its participants. We have the opportunity and power to do this.

Practice sutra: It is when your practice is greedy that you become discouraged with it. So you should be grateful that you have a sign or warning signal to show the weak point in your practice.

Osho (1999)

Summary

To practice the ethical way as a researcher, the Zen advice is to do no harm. In that respect qualitative researchers appreciate the IRB guidelines and follow them.

This chapter discussed lessons learned from examples of individual researchers and the IRB and the various misunderstandings they encountered. Confidentiality, anonymity, beneficence, respect for persons, and justice all align with doing no harm, which is the Zen approach to life. This chapter also put forth strategies for dealing with the IRB, including active communication with IRB members, gaining membership on the IRB, learning the rules and regulations of your local IRB, and doing a better job of explaining your work to the IRB. These strategies are needed especially when proposals are returned stating that interviewing is not research.

Mindful Activities

1. Do a library search for topics regarding ethics and qualitative research projects. Try key words such as "consent forms," "respect for persons," and "justice."

2. Make a copy of your institution's IRB consent form and rewrite it with the idea that a qualitative researcher is going to use this form in a new way. Be creative and think about the question, What would a consent form look like that addressed the needs of the qualitative researcher?

3. Prepare a reading list of books, key chapters, and articles on qualitative research methods and share it with your IRB members.

Suggested Resources for Further Understanding

Web Resources

www.irb.pitt.edu/

At this site, see the IRB email bulletin with such topics as:
— Ask the IRB
— Research Practice Fundamentals
— Research Involving Children

The site is user friendly and actually introduces the university IRB members to the university community.

www.hhs.gov/ohrp/

See this site for policy guidance, educational materials compliance oversight, and workshops. This site is from the Office for Human Research Protections, U.S. Department of Health and Human Services. It also provides interactive video training.

www.irbforum.org/

This site for the IRB Discussion and News Forum promotes discussion on ethics, regulations, problems, and policy regarding human subjects. It is a good teaching tool.

Journals that Regularly Focus on IRB Issues

Evaluation Review

Sample article: Oakes, J. M. (2002). Risks and wrongs in social science research: An evaluator's guide to the IRB. *26*(5), 443-479.

Ethics and Behavior

Sample article: Gunsalus, C. K. (2004). The nanny state meets the inner lawyer: Over-regulating while protecting human participants in research. *14*(4), 369-382.

Kennedy Institute of Ethics Journal
  Sample article: Holt, E. (2002). Expanding human research oversight. *12*(2), 215-224.

While these journals and sample articles capture some of the current discussion, the list is not meant to be exhaustive.

CHAPTER FIVE

Documents, Photographs, and Artifacts

He made it so simple and clear. It might take a long time
to catch the point.
If one realizes that it's stupid to search for fire with a lantern light,
the rice would not take so long to be done.

Rice koan

Documents as Data Using a Zen Approach

A Zen approach to documents, photographs, and artifacts encompasses consciousness, compassion, and creativity, as with any written word. Continuing with the frame of contemplative qualitative inquiry described in earlier chapters, we adjust to the document before us just as we would an interview transcript. I see documents, photographs, and any kind of artifacts as texts. They augment every story, interview, and observation and may actually serve to punctuate the meaning of a qualitative research project. I approach them as I would an interview transcript, for example. The same guidelines apply to using documents as to using interview transcripts and observational notes, and include the following.

1. Develop a rationale for the use of each document. How can the documents used in a given study contribute to its full meaning? Documents are a type of historical record from a given context of a social setting. Researchers selecting documents are faced with certain questions, such as Why am I selecting this document? What kind of language is used in the document and can it help illuminate my study? What might have

Valerie J. Janesick, "Documents, Photographs, and Artifacts" in *Contemplative Qualitative Inquiry: Practicing the Zen of Research*, pp. 81-89. © 2015 Left Coast Press, Inc. All rights reserved.

been the process in the construction of this document? Who controls the narrative?

2. Describe the document and its purpose. A document in written or photographic format or an artifact of any kind should be explained for the reader of the research project narrative. Again, acknowledge and be aware of the context for each document and any specifics related to the document and describe it fully.

3. Be clear about what type of document you are using in the study. Is it a public document? Is it personal, like the journal of a participant? Is it a visual document? Did you get permission to use the document? Public documents might include newspaper articles, academic articles and books, or novels, for example. Did you find the document on the Internet? If so, how did you check its authenticity? Visual documents might include photographs, video clips, video news segments, on line blogging, chats, websites, performances on YouTube, or any artwork or artifact.

4. Decide how you might organize, categorize, and make sense of each document after you create your list of documents. I like to use the framework described in Saldana's coding manual (2013). Begin with initial codes, which then become families of codes that are distilled into a category, with the various categories then becoming themes. In the past we often called this thematic analysis.

5. Find a way to make sense of your documents. I look at documents as a former choreographer and ask, as choreographers ask, Who is doing what, where, when, and why?

Once these steps are completed, the questions then become, Who wrote the document in the first place? Who controls the narrative in the document? What is the intent of the document? In whose best interest is this document? Where and when was the document created? What is its purpose or why was the document created in the first place? Why is it in use in this study?

Documents can add richness to any study, whether they are a curriculum vitae, a syllabus for a course, a public policy, a private letter, a notebook, a reflective journal entry, drawings, sketches, and/or emails. Even the posts collected while blogging become a series of documents in a study. Some journals today are dedicated to hard copy, whereas others are limited to online environments. For example, online avatars are being researched, gaming online is being studied, and as technology advances even further, I imagine that the sites for many more subjects will be available as "documents" for study.

Another use of documents is simply for providing detail and confirming accuracy. The letters, notes, and written official documents used in many projects provide a solid backdrop for checking many things. For example, in the 9/11 oral histories of New York City firefighters, the call sheets, phone logs, and lists of medications and onsite emergency services have helped the reader realize the social context of what was occurring at ground zero and nearby. Recently, the use of documents has come into prominence as part of qualitative data analysis. Altheide et al. (2008) have written extensively on emergent qualitative document analysis (QDA), sometimes also called Ethnographic Content Analysis (ECA).

In this chapter I discuss the use of QDA as a technique for augmenting the analysis and interpretation of oral histories. In document analysis it is helpful to focus on the content matter of the document and the interaction, if one exists, between the document and the participant in the oral history project. QDA is thought of as an orientation toward research. In many cases, it helps to make the past vividly connected to the present. Identifying themes and relationships that, for example, augment our understanding of a person's life is also part of analyzing documents. In an example that I use frequently, the student researcher provided many memos and documents from her previous and her current work. She chose to provide examples from her years of work in publishing and from her most recent career shift into the academic world. These documents were part of her portfolio of life, so to speak. Thus, for the oral historian, documents are an extension of the person, and they merit exploration in the search for understanding.

Photographs, Videos, and Other Online Data

For the qualitative researcher and the Zen practitioner, the film and online world awaits you. The appendices of this book provide examples of Zen lessons online in the form of applications (see Appendix B) and websites (see Appendix D), as well as a list of selected meditation centers (see Appendix C) and other resources (see Appendix E). The past decade has seen an abundance of resources available through the keyboard. In response to this growth, there are many books and journals on digital tools, free software, and other resources. In their dissertations and follow-up projects, doctoral students have effectively used photographs, video clips, and online sites, to name the key fixtures. Using one's own photographs, open-source photographs, blogs, and social media sites such as Pinterest, Facebook, or Twitter in qualitative research projects is now as common as writing with pen and paper.

In this arena, you have access to free software such as Express Scribe for assistance with transcribing interviews plus a multitude of market-driven software for data analysis at varying costs. Appendix F provides a sampler of digital tools useful in qualitative research projects. A quick survey of the Web will show that there are thousands of resources of this nature. Many journals in the fields of communication, sociology, and, recently, education welcome articles with photographs, documents, and artifacts, as long as they achieve the necessary rigor of qualitative research. This development means that you now have a rationale for using them in the study, as long as you explain their origin and context, and use a suitable approach to analyzing their content. Software on the market promises to do a great deal in terms of analysis, but in the end it is your creativity and ingenuity that work out the final analysis.

While interviewing is the major technique of most qualitative work and while journal writing as a research technique works well for many researchers to enrich a project, the importance of documents, artifacts, and photographs cannot be overstated. Documents enrich any study while capturing some portion of history. Spike Lee, the well known filmmaker, constructed a documentary film about Hurricane Katrina called *When the Levees Broke: A Requiem in Four Acts* that aired on the Home Box Office network (HBO). The film, which is four hours in length, includes interviews with various individuals who experienced the astounding events of Hurricane Katrina, as well as capturing the actual events in exquisite detail. The Rockefeller Foundation was so taken with the material in the film that it funded a project to teach citizens about New Orleans and the aftermath of Katrina, called *Teaching the Levees: A Curriculum for Democratic Dialogue and Civic Engagement*. The project was done in collaboration with Teacher's College, Columbia University. In addition to compact discs of the film, curriculum materials were developed around the subject of civic responsibility and rebuilding. This project provides a powerful example of using video to educate and inform not just the local population of New Orleans but also a wider audience of teachers and students, who may then carry the lessons on in their own histories as educators. When Spike Lee was interviewed in 2007 about the film and its purposes, he responded in this way:

One of the things I hope this documentary does is remind Americans that New Orleans is not over with, it's not done. Americans responded in record numbers to help the people of the Gulf Coast, but let's be honest. Americans have very, very short attention spans. And, I'll admit there was eventually a thing called Katrina fatigue. But if you go to New Orleans, only one-fourth of the population is there. People are still not home. So hopefully, this documentary will bring this fiasco, this travesty, back to the attention of the American people. And maybe the public can get some politicians' ass in the government to move quicker, and be more efficient in helping our fellow American citizens in the Gulf region.... I think when we look back on this many years from now, I'm confident that people are gonna see what happened in New Orleans as a defining moment in American history. Whether that's pro or con is yet to be determined. And that's one of the reasons why I wanted to do this film. (Crocco et al., 2007)

So much has been written about the power of the film and video in our lives that it almost goes without saying, once again, that qualitative researchers add to their knowledge base by using photographs, film, and video.

Photography

There is a growing body of literature on the use of photography as a research technique. Many websites today encourage the use of photography for documenting one's life story or a portion of it, through, for example, photographs of photos, wills, marriage certificates, artifacts, and documents such as a person's journal left for future generations.

One well known site that can be instructive is www.photovoice.org/, the website for PhotoVoice. This charitable organization encourages the use of documentary photography by helping those living on the margins of society to document their lives. Currently PhotoVoice has projects in twelve countries, pioneering the use of photography with refugees, children, orphans, the homeless, and HIV/AIDS victims. The locations include Macedonia, Russia, United Kingdom, Sri Lanka, Ethiopia, Cambodia, India, and Ecuador. Personnel consult with many NGOs such as foundations and UNICEF. The mission of PhotoVoice is to promote social justice and bring about positive social change. Members teach photography to individuals to enable them to document their lives and potentially generate income. PhotoVoice personnel are trying to sensitize the viewer to the plight of various outsiders, for example, the homeless.

Since we are constantly viewing visual images on the web, on television, in cinemas, and elsewhere, we risk experiencing saturation and, worse, indifference. Nevertheless, by using photography purposefully, we can more fully tell a story for those who will listen.

Archives as a Contemplative Site

Photography is often considered an archival strategy. Indeed, we can find many photographs and other documents in archives, making archives a good resource for many research projects.

Archival strategies are always valuable for the qualitative researcher in general and the oral historian in particular. For example, a narrative can be greatly enriched with either public or personal archival records. Public archives include libraries, tombstones, registries, hospital and police records, school records, commercial documents, and actuarial documents. Private documents include items and artifacts such as letters, notebooks, and photographs within documents. For more detailed information about archival documents, see the work of Lofland, Snow, Anderson, and Lofland (2006).

If you decide to do research at a library or archive center, find out first about the processes and rules. I am currently doing some archival research at the British Library in London, the world's largest research library. To use the library, I had to go through the application process to obtain a reader's card. I am examining letters of John Dewey to international educators. Some of the letters are not scanned, so I must wear gloves to read and review them. Also, no pens may be used in the library, only pencils, in order to protect the materials. Archives are very much alive, just as meditation is alive and active.

We now have access to large amounts of information through the use of technology, and many archival documents are ours for the asking. I use documents in class to give students a chance to find themes or to write poetry about what is in the document. This exercise gets the thought process going and uses more than one part of the brain. See, for example, the following example of a document, in this case a press release, and the resulting poems about it to imagine ways of representing data from a document source. Documents come to life through writing about them and through writing poetry about them. I encourage students and other researchers in training to use as many art forms as possible, at any time or even as part of their final dissertation defense.

> *Zazen sutra*: When we sit zazen, seated and walking Zen meditation, the eyes are kept open. This is most important. In Zen, one is not escaping reality. Rather, one is encountering it in the most intimate way.
>
> *Ford, (2002)*

Example of a Public Document:
Press Release Regarding Donation

by the National Audubon Society

TAMPA, Fla. (June 25, 2014) - The graceful herons and spoonbills that call Florida home are the living legacy of a small group of people who were responsible for some of the 20th century's most heroic conservation efforts.

A collection of journals and logbooks donated to the USF Tampa Library Special Collections by the National Audubon Society is providing a rare and valuable glimpse into early endeavors to save threatened bird populations at a time when conservation was not a priority for most Floridians.

Today we've become accustomed to the sight of blue herons fishing on the shoreline and ibises strolling through vegetation. But according to the documents, countless birds nearly became extinct in the early 1900s, when hunters sought to procure their elegant plumage.

Assistant Librarian Andy Huse calls the collection a "treasure trove" that sheds much-needed light on the intense conservation work that saved bird colonies in Florida and other regions, including numerous wading bird species that were on the brink of extinction.

As discussed in Chapter 7, in addition to the traditional approaches described earlier, poetry is another approach for capturing the meaning of any document. One way to use poetry is to provoke an idea or provoke a discussion. The following haiku are my reactions to the photos that accompanied the preceding press release and that captured a heron and a roseate spoonbill.

The Heron

The heron waltzes along
In the photo eyeing me
As if she had something to laugh about.

Spoonbill

The spoonbill lifts one leg
So effortlessly
It must be the start of a ballet.

Treasure Trove

Once nearly extinct
The great blue heron and ibis dazzle us today.
Keep them safe Audubon Society.
They are a treasure trove.

Our work comes alive and takes on new importance when, as qualitative researchers, we use documents, artifacts, photographs, blogs, and social media excerpts to make a point creatively. Use these effectively, and your narrative, that is, the story of your participants' lives, may sparkle just a bit more. Documents, artifacts, and photographs offer us a wealth of possibilities for interpretation and meaning.

Summary

This chapter discussed the potential of documents, photographs, and artifacts to add to the breadth of contemplative qualitative inquiry. Using a Zen approach is to think of new ways to view documents, artifacts, and photographs. An example of a public document was included to demonstrate that poetry might be a way to interpret documents. Any photographs or artifacts in your study are food for analysis, interpretation, and meaning. They become another data set to round out your final narrative.

Mindful Activities

1. Create a PowerPoint presentation teaching your peers about storytelling in any of its forms.
2. Find a blog on qualitative research. Respond to at least three of the postings and share the blog with your peers.
3. Photograph a portion of your environment, and write two pages about the photographs.
4. Find a public document and attempt to explain it in one paragraph. Next, try writing a poem about the meaning of the document.

Suggested Resources for Further Understanding

For Qualitative Research Methods

Paulus, T. M., Lester, J. N., & Dempster, P. G. (2014). *Digital tools for qualitative researchers*. Thousand Oaks, CA: Sage.

Pink, S. (2006) *The future of visual anthropology: Engaging the senses*. New York: Routledge.

CHAPTER SIX

Nirvana and Writing Up Qualitative Research

In early times in Japan, bamboo and paper lanterns were used with candles inside. A blind man visiting a friend one night was offered a lantern to guide him home. "I do not need a lantern. Darkness or light is the same to me." His friend said, "Yes, I know, but if you do not have a lantern, someone may run into you." The blind man started off with the lantern. Just then someone ran into him. "Watch where you are going! Can't you see this lantern?" To this, the man replied, "Brother, your candle has burned out."

Teaching the Ultimate koan

Introduction

Perhaps the most misunderstood concept of Zen is that of Nirvana. Nirvana is used to refer to the state of absolute bliss achieved when an individual comes to enlightenment, which means that the person has realized the power of non-self and impermanence. In addition, it means that the person is fully awakened to the world. In other words, the self is an illusion. The idea of nirvana also includes the elimination of all pain and all concerns about birth and death. As we look into our impermanent self, we realize we are simply not separate people. Our ancestors are in us, our teachers are in us, and the past is in us, here and now. As the Buddhist teacher Thich Nhat Hanh reminds us, if we meditate by looking at orange blossoms, for example, we also see the oranges because we know what the blossoms signify. In that sense, nirvana encompasses the future as well. Nirvana is often described as utter and complete peace due to the cessation of suffering, pain, and desire for things we do not need. Nirvana is total liberation and enlightenment. The concept of nirvana can be useful to qualitative researchers, because, all components of our studies include the past, the present, and the future. Our goal is to get to the heart of the subject matter and enlighten others about the lived experience of our participants. At the same time, we as researchers need to have a deep understanding of who we are at the time of the study. In order to describe our role in the study, we are always in the process of understanding our place in it and developing new points of view from working with our participants. This is nirvana. Exploring new points of view is part of becoming aware and enlightened.

I often use principles of choreography and the arts, my favorite metaphors, as frames in my writing. These principles—design, balance, composition, and harmony—can also be applied to contemplative qualitative inquiry, using the following questions.

Design: Is the story we tell and write about cohesive and coherent?

Balance: Is the story trustworthy and believable?

Composition: Are the roles of the researcher and participant clearly described and all ethical considerations revealed?

Harmony: Are the conclusions and interpretations based on the data presented in the study? Is there a meaningful story with nuance and texture including an aesthetic component? Are we able to write in an engaging and joyful manner?

Let us now examine these questions to assist us in understanding how to make sense of our techniques and practices as qualitative researchers and in using this understanding to inform our writing.

1. Design

The qualitative researcher asks: Is the story cohesive and coherent?

The Zen teacher asks: What exactly is this story?

Cohesiveness relates to the formal conventions of writing for publication such as the style used, which in our case is set out in the sixth edition of the *Publication Manual of the American Psychology Association* (2010). Great care must be taken with language and how it is used.

Few people will read the account of a life if it is not structurally, artfully, and beautifully written. The aesthetic component of writing is crucial. Using poetry, photographs, drawing, or artwork should be considered a way to complement the written narrative. Technology such as Wordle or Tagxedo, which creates a visual picture from words, would surely add an aesthetic touch. Quotations of participants' words, drawn from the transcripts of interviews, are also important and are often the mainstay of the story.

In addition, as the researcher/writer of the qualitative research study, you need to present the case with sensitivity to meaning. What did the participant mean in this or that sentence? If media other than words are used to portray the story, are these media authentic and how are they integrated into the story? To do this kind of work, you need to become a skilled writer and interpreter. For example, it is important to interpret any colloquialisms, metaphors, language, slang, humor, and stereotypes from a participant in an interview or document. Other details also affect the meaning. The recent biography of Cleopatra (Schiff, 2010) is written with great attention to the detail of Cleopatra's time period. The gender issues of the day and the role of a powerful female leader are all described in the appropriate historical context. Other writers in the genre of biography and personal stories also capture the context of the time period in details of the life story, and then make meaning of those data. You are both scientist and artist in one. In terms of presentation of the data, their meaning, and their interpretation, your task is to create a compelling narrative that carries the reader along. In addition, and obviously, this kind of writing demands an audience, so you should know your audience before you start writing and then write for that audience.

Furthermore, cohesiveness is connected to coherence, in particular to methodological coherence. The title of the work should reflect the story presented. The abstract of the work should summarize the same purpose, techniques, and conclusions promised in the title and delivered in the body of the work. The research questions must be suited to the methodology. The presentation of data, analysis of data, and interpretation of the analysis should follow from the research questions and methodology. An effective final report gets to the heart of the story, and so designing the story coherently, like writing poetry, is pivotal and substantial to the writing process. Using a Zen view, learning the basics is the first step toward achieving nirvana.

2. Balance

The qualitative researcher asks: Is the story told trustworthy and believable?

The Zen teacher asks: Who are you?

Although many writers have written about trustworthiness, I focus here on the writings of Herbert and Irene Rubin (2005) and on my own work (Janesick, 2011). Throughout the long and elegant history of qualitative work, many checks and balances have been established to ensure trustworthiness. For one thing, qualitative researchers must hold to the ethical codes of conduct of a given discipline. Also, the IRBs of all institutions follow the federal requirements and may add additional requirements if working with protected populations.

Some unwritten rules of qualitative research also serve as balancing mechanisms. Zen is concerned with balance. Thus you might ask the following questions.

1. *Did the researcher study her own group or a group where hierarchical relationships are or were present?*

   If, for example, as a doctoral student, you wish to study perspectives on teaching by collecting life histories of teachers, using members of your faculty as the study participants may incur unneeded conflicts of interest or interactional headaches later on. IRB members look with concern on this mixing of the roles of practitioner and researcher. There are plenty of teachers who will be happy to tell their stories who are not in your current lifeworld. If you choose to work in a setting that is too close to home, this decision could haunt you. For example, what would happen if a participant later denied saying something or had a falling out with you? What one says in one's youth may not be one's opinion or belief later on in life, but, living in a digital era when blogs and social network statements can serve as data, such statements may be captured permanently. The digital generation admits there is no privacy, but there still are many who wish to keep some things private, especially with regard to sensitive topics such as race, class, gender, and power. A good way to handle this concern is to make explicit your role as the researcher somewhere in the final reporting of the project.

2. *Did the researcher use an outside reader?*

Many researchers in the traditions of qualitative research use an outside reader of field notes, transcripts, and initial categories and codes to provide a critical sounding board. There are many study groups and writing feedback groups on the Web, if you cannot get feedback from a peer or colleague.

3. *Did the researcher do member checks, that is, have the participants seen the data and/or the final write up of the research?*

   This technique is valuable for ensuring that the story being told is believable and trustworthy.

4. *Is the study designed to understand a person's life?*

   A good example of long-term case studies is the work of Oliver Sacks (1995). As he takes the reader through rare and paradoxical life histories, there is no mistaking the fact that Sacks writes to understand the lived experience and make sense of it. This work contrasts with other approaches designed for prediction and control. Another superb example of a powerful life history is Henrietta Lacks' story, as told by Rebecca Skloot (2011) in her book *The Immortal Life of Henrietta Lacks*. Skloot studied this case for over a decade and used interviews, documents, and formal notes to record Lacks' journey.

5. *Was enough time spent in the field or in reviewing documents?*

   Does this study entail enough time in the research process to warrant the conclusions and interpretations presented? A good rule is that time in the field needs equal or more time in analysis. In our fast paced world, this succinct rule of thumb from the history of more than one discipline is a good one for us to follow.

6. *Have all points of tension and conflict been uncovered?*

   It is always wise to look for points of tension and conflict, that is, data that do not ring true or are biased. A one-sided report does not convince the reader. Keep track of the points of tension and challenges in your study in your researcher reflective journal.

7. *Has a pilot study been completed?*

   Another important undertaking is the faithful and steadfast pilot study. Doing a pilot study can save a great deal of time later in the study. I cannot say too much about the need to test your interview questions and methods of observation in the field, double checking your reflections through the researcher reflective journal and trying out initial themes, categories, and/or codes. This step alone will improve your confidence in the entire design and conduct of the research. The pilot study assists researchers by testing the interview questions. It also provides a forum for redesigning parts of the study, including the interview questions. Time after time students mention the value of the pilot study, and I encourage writing about it in the final report. The more comprehensive your written work, the more it will be understood.

8. *Have ethical issues been addressed as needed?*

All matters that are potential ethical issues must be addressed in the final reporting. For example, in a recent dissertation study, a participant became tired of the interviews and dropped out. The researcher then wrote a small section on the implications of this resignation, viewing it as an ethical issue. Likewise, before a study is undertaken, all consent forms must be current and appropriate clearance must be obtained. Above all, the rule of doing no harm is ever present in any qualitative study.

In addition, consider the points made by Rubin and Rubin (2012). They cite thoroughness, believability, and transparency as important checks and balances for any given narrative. Achieving these qualities ensures that the story is well rounded. In my work in life history and oral history, I often record people's stories of trauma and critical events that changed their views on life. For example, immediately following traumatic events such as 9/11 and Hurricane Katrina, the focus of these stories is often on the immediacy of the event, but when one steps back to look at the big picture contextually, the stories reveal many layers about the people being interviewed. They carry trustworthiness through the experience of the trauma and, from this quality, a sense of empowerment evolves.

As I have written recently (Janesick, 2010), describing experience or a set of experiences provides a sense of history that serves to illuminate the present situation. It also helps our work to be Zen like. Qualitative research enables you to describe precisely much of what you are doing as a qualitative researcher. A story is always connected to some piece of history, much like the historical legacy of Zen or the historical legacy of the written word. Acknowledging this sense of history when we write up a story empowers us with respect for other stories and other points of view. These stories, unlike our own, enable us to see additional interpretations of the social world and our experience with it. Along with the points made earlier in this section, this insight brings us to trustworthiness. Our personal histories have to do with our ancestors and their ancestors. The compelling requirement of transparency is a component in leading us to acknowledge our sense of history and thus to improve our trustworthiness. This is a Zen like approach.

3. Composition

> *The qualitative researcher asks:* Are the roles of the researcher and participant clearly described and all ethical considerations revealed?
>
> *The Zen teacher asks:* Can you ensure you will do no harm?

Over the past five decades, when there was criticism of qualitative work in general, it was routinely said that qualitative researchers need to be more explicit about the design of the study, the methodology used throughout the study, the rationale for the selection of partici-pants, and the relationship between the researcher and the participant. I wholeheartedly agree. In fact, it would be helpful for all researchers to more fully explain the process of their research projects. The more we can be clear, descriptive, and forthcoming about these matters, the better the state of the art. When I started conducting oral histories, initially for a lengthy project involving female leaders, I was surprised to learn that oral history projects are not considered research by certain bureaucrats. Federal government overseers state emphatically that the findings of oral history projects are not suitable for generalizing and therefore that such projects are not research. Specifically, the U.S. Office for Human Research Protections (OHRP), which is part of the U.S. Department of Health and Human Services (HHS), has determined that oral history interview projects do not involve the type of research defined by HHS regulations and therefore are excluded from IRB oversight (see Part 46 of the OHRP Code of Federal Regulations).

The American Historical Association (AHA) has a lengthy state-ment on this proclamation. To summarize the AHA statement briefly, federal regulations have a definition of research that includes general-izability. Since one's lived experience is unique and all individual stories are just that, oral history is not included as research. Other research approaches similar to oral history are also underserved by this ruling. Life history, biography, autobiography, and autoethnography are included in the group that is not considered research. At my current institution, for example, several students who sent IRB applications for life history projects were told that IRB approval was not required as their work was not research. The students replied that it was research, described why it was, asked for an expedited review, and ultimately obtained approvals. My guess is that the IRB decided it was easier to approve their proposals than go through several back-and-forth questions and replies. Several universities and professional historical societies have debated this issue, and it is well documented in the literature, with summaries available on the websites of the Oral History Association and the American Historical Association. Some universities require IRB approval for oral histories and similar research approaches, whereas others elect not to; both sides offer strong and credible arguments. Consequently, there is a considerable elasticity in interpretation of the need to seek IRB approval. For dissertations and theses, however, no matter what the research approach, completing the form and obtaining IRB approval is important, if for no other reason than achieving compliance with graduate studies procedures and, of course, to educate IRB members.

As you might expect, institutions vary as to how they interpret the federal regulations. Professional organizations have also weighed in on the subject. In this chapter I do not talk about the conflicting conceptions of qualitative research. That discussion is available in many textbooks, journals, proceedings of annual meetings of professional organizations, and so on. Interestingly, the original federal regulations for IRBs were set up for medicine, which employs a different approach to research, although, ironically, it also involves individual cases. Regardless, my point here is that qualitative researchers should err on the side of safety and be sure that informed consent is obtained in any research project. Oral history in particular offers a fascinating situation: the people interviewed are not anonymous, and the power of documenting a story holds great appeal. Unfortunately, many legal scholars have argued that oral history is like journalism, in that it tells one person's story, and only that. Further, in our multimedia age, there is a sense in journalism that anything goes.

One has only to look at YouTube to see this idea played out. In contrast, oral history, as an academic discipline, has always held to the requirement of obtaining informed consent from interviewees before reproducing their words or any photographs, videos, or documents used in a story. As oral historians we may be perplexed by the IRB requirements but we have always used consent forms. Nevertheless, for any qualitative research project involving interviews it is always wise to seek an expedited IRB review for purposes of ethical and humane considerations. Furthermore, for dissertations and theses, which typically are the first step in a research career, these projects obviously should have IRB approval. Finally, as I argued earlier in this book, I see the role of qualitative researchers as one which includes educating IRB members about our work.

An additional ethical issue that emerges in this postmodern era is that of social justice in and throughout the research process. Viewing research projects involving interviews as a social justice process gives one the opportunity to look at the stories of individuals usually excluded from mainstream research. By documenting these stories, we get a fuller picture of the life and practices of society. For example, Venkatesh (2008) in his study of gangs in Chicago used a combination of the life history of a gang leader and ethnography to examine what it means to be a member of a gang through the lens of critical theory. Among other questions, Venkatesh tried to determine what policies help some people and not others. By shadowing a gang leader, interviewing him, and, in fact, taking on the role of gang leader for a day, this researcher deconstructed theories on the hierarchies in this sub-society, its relationship to some public policy implementation, how gangs function in a neighborhood, and the personal leadership struggle of a gang leader reflecting values of the community itself. He also exposed the graft and corruption in the Chicago Housing Authority as part of the story, and, in an ironic way, described and explained the many injustices that lead to social justice. In this example, life history and biography become vehicles for enriching the knowledge base of both qualitative research methods and social justice. By expanding our research to include stories of individuals outside the usual stream of participants and on the margins of society, we can make readers more aware of the complete picture of society.

In the postmodern study of people and their stories, interviews of persons generally on the outside or periphery of society offer a unique opportunity to document and record many ways of the world. Women, minorities, people labeled as disabled, and anyone who is categorized as "the other," or at least not a member of the mainstream, may benefit from actually recording their stories. Given that this social justice record is preserved, the stories cannot be lost. As we trace someone's life journey, or a portion of it, up to the present, qualitative researchers may find a way to analyze and interpret these stories in a way that advances social justice.

One of the useful prototypes of this genre of research is testimony, a research technique used by many qualitative researchers over the history of our craft. As a key component of life history, oral history, autoethnography, testimony, and biography, testimony provides us with an avenue of thick description, analysis, and interpretation of people's lives through probing the past and present. Globally, testimony has been used to document the stories of victims and the perpetrators who committed crimes against them. Such testimony provides a written record of a catalogue of misdeeds that can then facilitate some aspect of social justice. For example, the Truth and Reconciliation Commission (TRC) was a vehicle for capturing the witnesses' stories of the events occurring in South Africa under the earlier system of apartheid. Testimony allowed all of us to more fully understand the political, cultural, emotional, and psychological aspects of apartheid as never before. Storytelling is part of the African culture, and the brave individuals who took part in the TRC process gave straightforward descriptions, often emotional and jarring, of what had occurred. Their testimony was the first step toward forgiveness and reconciliation. Desmond Tutu (1999) has argued that one cannot arrive at forgiveness without truth as a starting point. Tutu and other writers often catalogue four types of truth as follows:

1. factual and forensic truth, that is, evidence of what actually occurred;

2. personal or narrative truth, that is, the person's story of how something occurred;

3. social or cultural truth, which is basically the social context and history of what occurred; and

4. healing or restorative truth, that is, what is needed to heal the wounds of the three previously listed types of truth. This type of truth is very much like the Zen notion of compassion for all living things.

Disciplines that are practice based, for example, education, nursing, business, medical studies, health, and social work, stand to benefit immensely from using testimony. In conducting qualitative research projects involving members of groups typically outside the mainstream, we have chosen an effective way to document society's injustice, cruelty, and thoughtlessness. Testimony, in any format, furthers our knowledge of the lived experience of any number of individuals on the edges of society. Using testimony to promote social justice awareness can assist us in achieving a more rigorous and inclusive practice. It can also serve to illuminate our roles as researchers and advance our field of research.

4. Harmony

The qualitative researcher asks: Are the conclusions and interpretations based on the data and is the narrative coherent, nuanced, and layered? Are the voices of marginalized individuals included? Are aesthetic components present?

The Zen teacher asks: Is there anything you wish to or need to say about Zen?

Any research report needs to convince the reader of its meaning, both in the details that shape the story and the overall implications of the work. In this type of work, as in the arts, context is everything. Qualitative researchers need to be persuasive writers. By laying out the details of the story, the thick description that sets the scene, and the words of the participants, we have the beginning of the documentation of lived experience. But what do we do with these details? Here we come to the crux of writing up the story to be told. Today, in this postmodern endeavor—and by "postmodern" I refer here to research that examines race, class, gender, and power—many media and many approaches are available to create new ways of representing the data. Chapter 7 discusses two of these approaches, found data poems and identity poetry, which are often part of performance research.

Performance research may include digital video stories, drama, poetry, and any other performance medium. YouTube is a source of hundreds of examples. By including an aesthetic component in the final reporting of our research, we stand to attract more readers, for example, digital natives. Digital natives are people who, since early childhood, have grown up using technology and expecting it to work for them. In addition, by including an aesthetic component, we round out our humanity. Why would we exclude it? It encourages the nirvana-like quality of becoming awakened. I am reminded of the well known anonymous statement, again very Zen like, "All things pass, art alone endures."

Since we live in a digitally saturated environment, students are often digital natives and generally prefer digital formats. Indeed, they think digitally. It makes sense to cater to this strength in the representation of qualitative research data. Large collections of video archives in story formats are stored online and, of course, on YouTube. In a recent search on Google using the terms "qualitative research" and "interviews," nearly 600,000 items popped up. On the Internet, one can find straightforward interviews on video with graphics overlaid for extracting meaning, photo montages overlaid with a narrator, and many other performance examples to get one thinking about new ways of representing lived experience. In addition, some qualitative researchers are telling their own stories online as autobiographies. By using the digital tools available to us all, we can now create a space and keep it forever on a public-forum site, YouTube. What is also striking about this new approach to data presentation is the obvious visual space for all voices to be included. Thus, a social justice theme is ever present. In terms of achieving harmony, we need to be aware of and include all voices. In the education literature, this approach is called anti-oppression pedagogy. Included in the notion of nirvana, first, there is enlightenment and harmony. Also included is the notion of anti-oppression. This idea refers back to the Zen concept of non-self: for Zen to become active in a person, that person must understand that all of us are connected as part of the universe. Everything is seen as one.

Go to the center sutra

In Zen, the answer always lies in being more centered.
That is where everything blossoms.
The more we stay at the periphery,
The more we are spun out as the wheel of life turns.
But when we go to the center,
We ride the turn of the wheel without tension.

Writing as an Act of Joy and Mindfulness

Thinking about writing as an act of joy and mindfulness has always been part of my approach to writing and to teaching about writing. Since storytelling is the essence of qualitative research, writing is of prime concern. Qualitative work relies on documenting the stories of lived experiences from all walks of society. Debates are always present about the purposes of research, and many qualitative researchers contribute to an understanding of research as well as contributing to social justice. Some argue for changing the inequities of the status quo through well designed qualitative studies. In my view, quality, quantity, and the joy of writing assist in any storytelling and often contribute to the record of social justice. If we can write, as Stephen King (2002) suggests so competently, we become part of a history of storytellers and, intentionally or not, end up contributing to a social justice record, depending on the types of questions that we ask.

Writing with joy poses a few questions. Does the writing capture the lived experience to the extent that the reader feels that he or she is walking in the interviewee's shoes? Does the story capture the whole picture, warts and all? What doesn't seem to fit—the ruptures, so to speak—are often as important as the smooth sets of words and pictures. Derrida (1972) pointed out that when we try to capture a person's life story in any form, we always filter it through the hidden meanings of language, and thus our work is always unstable as all languages are in flux. In this context, I consider the digital and the poetic as languages. I do not think this filter should deter us from trying to capture the lived experience of our participants. Qualitative methods are time tested and rigorous. These methods include interviews, documents, the research reflective journal, and observation, and they reveal all the concerns of the postmodern researcher such as race, class, and gender issues. They force us to experience other ways of knowing. Basically we are researching subjectivity and we are proud of that. We welcome documenting the rigor of the process, and we embrace the ambiguities and contradictions in anyone's story. We, as researchers, tell the entire story, as best as we can with our level of expertise. We are narrative writers. We begin with an idea that seizes us. Stephen King (2000) points out in his famous book *On Writing* that, when he recalls his first writing, he remembers that the idea of writing a story came with an immense feeling of possibility. He felt as if he had been ushered into a building filled with closed doors and had been given leave to open any door he liked. He then describes the two theses of his book.

I approached this book using King's two theses, both simple. The first is that good writing consists of mastering the fundamentals (vocabulary, grammar, and the elements of style) and then filling your tool box with the right instruments. The second thesis is that, while it is impossible to make a competent writer out of a bad writer, and while it is equally impossible to make a great writer our of a good one, it is possible, with lots of hard work, dedication, and timely help, to make a good writer out of a competent one (King, 2000, p.142). Thus, we strive to become more competent, to be more aware of working toward excellence in our writing, and this goal can be reached most often by practice, just as in Zen meditation. Practice makes perfect, as the saying goes. Quantity and quality of writing must go together; they are the yin and yang of writing. Nothing can substitute for the practice of writing, just as nothing can substitute for the practice of thinking and meditation.

When you think about your favorite fiction and non-fiction writers, what comes across in their writing? For me, it is the sheer joy of it. The glee and euphoria that comes with writing shines through. Similarly, for me, the joy of writing overrides all the long hours, the highs and lows of the writing process, and the demands of rewriting. A major component of writing is rewriting. Without it, where would we all be as writers? Likewise, where would we all be without feedback? Writing is a process that relies on both rewriting and feedback. They take us to a higher level in the quantity and quality of our writing.

Others have also written about the joy in writing. Natalie Goldberg (2005), in her classic book *Writing Down the Bones: Freeing the Writer Within,* offers ideas that can benefit us all. She suggests:

> Don't make your mind do anything. Simply step out of the way and record your thoughts as they roll through you. Writing practice softens the heart and mind, helps to keep us flexible so that rigid distractions between apples and milk, tigers and celery disappear.... You will take leaps naturally if you follow your thoughts, because the mind takes great leaps. Have you ever been able to just stay with one thought? Another one arises. (p. 37)

I equate the joy of writing to the state of nirvana, or arriving at wide awakedness. The Zen objective of getting to mindfulness is part of nirvana. Through being mindful of our connectedness to our participants, the culture we are part of, and our non-self, we move toward the awareness that is part of nirvana.

Research for Social Justice

A number of discussions and debates have been taking place in research forums and conferences about the topic of research for social justice. One example is How can we include marginalized individuals in research projects? The Zen concept of doing no harm certainly resonates with social justice as an aim for life and for research. Imbedded in this notion is the intention to try and diminish oppressive practices, or at least speak out against them, once we know that harm is being done. Zen concepts of compassion and loving kindness resonate with this approach for the simple reason that loving kindness is an antidote to oppressive practices. Medical researchers and social workers have always led the way in discussions of this topic. Currently, in the social sciences, we are aware of the need for anti-oppressive practices not only in education but also in all research projects. These practices help to round out the research practice as a whole, moving us toward the realization of impermanence, non-self, and nirvana. As a result, we become enlightened. We experience moments of nirvana.

Summary

Nirvana is defined as a transcendent state of mind wherein all concepts of pain and suffering are extinguished. It implies learning a new point of view. Many meditation teachers liken nirvana to water as the basis of all things Buddhist. Water is the stuff of life and the stuff of the universe. In Zen Buddhism, nirvana is the state of awareness, being wide awake to living in this present beautiful moment. Nirvana implies complete agreement with the universe and knowing one's place within it, connected to people and the natural world. For the qualitative researcher, this component of the metaphor of Zen can be viewed as the point when we achieve understanding and awaken to the meaning of our final reporting of the study. Furthermore, it implies experiencing joy during the process of writing up the study and making it meaningful to the readers of our research. Writing is mindfulness in a sense, and mindfulness gives us a slice of nirvana. Finally, doing research for social justice includes doing no harm, a sense of compassion and loving kindness, but it also implies stopping oppressive practices. This is Zen in the qualitative research world.

Mindful Moment: One of the meditations throughout the history of meditation is that of the gratitude meditation. It goes something like this. Think of all the people, places, and things you are grateful for and experience gratitude in your heart, soul, mind and being. Enumerate each of them while saying I am grateful for (name them). Then release all toxic feelings as you experience gratitude once again.

Mindful Activities

1. Write the history of your writing. Make a timeline, beginning with your very first memory of writing. Was it a note to Santa? Did you keep a diary? Start from whatever was your first experience of writing, and chronicle your progress to the present. Notice whether there were key moments when your writing changed and what types of writing you experienced. Now, write a page or more describing the type of writer you are today and how you got there.

2. Set up a quiet area in your living space and create writing goals for yourself, for example, to write one page in your journal every morning. To start, you might recall your previous day and write about it. One of my teachers once told me that, if you claim to be a writer, you should write every day. Begin by writing down all the things and people in your life that you are grateful for.

3. Time yourself for fifteen minutes of writing. Sit down and write like crazy. Commit to the fifteen minutes. Do not worry about what you are writing. Just write about something, for example, your favorite meal or the meaning of friendship. Write, stop, and then read what you wrote. You will be amazed at how much you can do in fifteen minutes.

Suggested Resources for Further Understanding

Literally, there are thousands of journal articles, books, and YouTube videos on qualitative research methods, meditation methods, and Zen. I have selected the following texts for their nuance, texture, and layers of understanding. Also, the authors have spent a lifetime doing this work and following a given tradition.

About Qualitative Methods

Clandinin, D. J. & Connelly, M. (2000). *Narrative inquiry: Experience and story in qualitative research.* San Francisco, CA: Jossey-Bass.

Cole, A. L. & Knowles, J. G. (2001). *Lives in context: The art of life history research.* New York: Alta Mira Press.

Denzin, N. (1997). *Interpretive ethnography.* Thousand Oaks, CA: Sage.

Ellis, C. & Flaherty, M. (Eds.). (1992). *Investigating subjectivity: Research on lived experience.* Thousand Oaks, CA: Sage.

Goldberg, N. (2005). *Writing down the bones.* Boston: Shambala Press.

Hess-Biber, S. N. & Leavy, P. (Eds.). (2008). *Handbook of emergent methods.* New York: Guilford Press.

Jones, S. H., Adams, T., & Ellis, C. (Eds.). (2013). *Handbook of autoethnography.* Walnut Creek, CA: Left Coast Press, Inc.

Leavy, P. (Ed.). (2014). *The Oxford handbook of qualitative research.* New York: Oxford University Press.

Rubin, H. J. & Rubin, I. S. (2005). *Qualitative interviewing: The art of hearing data,* (2nd ed.). Thousand Oaks, CA: Sage.

About Zen

Levin, D. (2009). *Zen life: An open-at-random book of guidance.* Pittsburgh, PA: St. Lynn's Press.

CHAPTER SEVEN

Poetry, Zen, and Qualitative Research

When Banzan was walking through a market he overheard a conversation between a butcher and his customer. "Give me the best piece of meat you have," said the customer. "Everything in my shop is the best," replied the butcher. "You cannot find here any piece of meat that is not the best." At these words Banzan became enlightened.

Everything is Best koan

Introduction

Zen and poetry go together historically and in the present time. Poetry has always been a part of Zen teaching, as poetry gets to the essence of an idea or thought. In particular haiku and other Japanese forms of poetry are used as a guide in meditation or following meditation, and may be written by the meditator. Early Zen practitioners were connected to nature more directly and profoundly than today's learners. The rituals of awaking early and writing poems about dawn, sunrise, sunset, flora, and fauna are found in Zen poetry. Indeed, haiku began with a solid focus on the natural world.

Recently, qualitative researchers have been using poetry to represent theory, literature reviews, data analysis, and interpretations. In this chapter, poetry is promoted as a strategy for best practices in qualitative research methods, following from the example of Zen poetry. Historically, Zen teachers often gave instructions that each student should write a verse or poem at the start of learning meditation practice. Through this strategy, the Zen teacher could assess the level of understanding of that student. Of course, today, many students are reluctant to attempt to write a poem, and so the teacher often gives them a written example and lets the learner read and reread the poem to gain confidence to write an original poem. This is a treasured and valuable Zen practice. It is a tradition for head monks or teachers to provide examples like this. From as early as the eighth century CE there is written documentation of poetry as part of Zen teaching. Watson (2009) offers a full description of Zen poetry and its history. For example, see the following poem written about that time by the head teacher/monk Shen-hsiu in China, as taken from Watson's book.

> The body is the tree of wisdom,
> The mind a bright mirror on its stand.
> At all times take care to keep it polished
> Never let the dust and grime collect.

Realize that many students at that time did not know how to write and often went to the head teacher for assistance. In this case, a student, Hui-neng, responded as follows.

> Wisdom never had a tree
> The bright mirror lacks a stand.
> There never was anything to begin with
> Where could the dust and grime collect?

After reading this insightful poem, the head teacher handed over his robes to the student.

This Chinese tradition uses poetry consisting of four lines, some rhymes, and a certain number of syllables in Chinese. Bear in mind that there are many variations in form as a result of translations into English from any number of the Asian languages. Regardless, the key idea here is the importance of poetry as part of everyday life, including, for me, the everyday life of the qualitative researcher.

Poetry as a form of inquiry and thought is gaining ground in the social sciences, as evidenced by the recently growing literature on poetry and qualitative research (Barone, 2004; Feldman, 2004; Leavy 2009). The most used poetic form is *found data poetry*. Found data poems are exactly that: found. They are poems found in interview transcripts, in documents from the research site, in performances, and in any text relevant to the research project. For example, someone's resume, emails, policy documents, participants' written statements, or reflective research journals may be fodder for a found data poem. Many in the field of arts based research (ABR) have led the way in describing and validating poetry as a form of inquiry (see, for example, Barone, 2001). Of all the art forms, poetry is most suited to representing the mind. Another type of Zen poetry is Japanese *death poetry*, which is the poetry of Zen monks and haiku poets at the verge of death. In Japan, many individuals, as they near death, reflect upon their lives and write poems for their families and friends. What we learn from this genre is how important poetry was then, and still is, in the Zen frame. It provides a powerful lesson for qualitative researchers. The practice of writing poetry is ingrained in Zen and can be a part of the qualitative researcher's tool kit as well.

Why Poetry?

Poetry is a dynamic way of representing thinking and emotions. Poetry allows you to participate in something—an idea, a feeling, a reality. Poetry invites engagement; you cannot be a bystander when a poem crashes into you. It is a democratic form as well, since anyone and everyone may write a poem. For qualitative researchers, poetry challenges traditional ways of thinking. Like any art form, it is able to jar us into thinking in new directions. Furthermore, there is a lyrical and beautiful quality to poetry that is sorely needed in research. In addition, poetry makes the cleanest and most pithy use of words. There is little confusion in poetry. Poets get to the heart of the matter. Poetry maximizes meaning. Poetry forces us to think in new ways, as a Zen teacher teaches us to do in meditation. Poetry is important for the qualitative researcher, because we look at the experience of our participants and want to render that experience in many forms. When we tell someone's story, we create a poetic sense oftentimes. By using found data poems, for example, we can accomplish a great deal.

Poetry provides a way to empower each of us as qualitative researchers as well as our participants. Also, poetry may illuminate a situation, a context, or a series of positive or negative events. In addition, poetry forces us to make sense of our world in a new and fresh way. It forces us to see in a futuristic way. Poetry shuts out the excess and the noise. It inspires an awareness of and respect for other people's stories, which is critical for the qualitative researcher. Poetry has a long tradition and history in literature and the arts. Currently, there is a great deal of interest in using poetry in social science research, and it could not have come at a better time (see Appendix E).

As Eisner (2004) mentions, the ways we represent things eventually have an effect on how we perceive them and, of course, how we make meaning of them.

> There is no single legitimate way to make sense of the world. Different ways of seeing give us different worlds. Different ways of saying, allow us to represent different worlds. A novel as well as a statistical mean can enlarge human understanding. (p. 33)

In other words, one size does not fit all. In fact, one size fits few. In this day of high stakes testing in education, entertainment in place of news, and preoccupation with celebrities, it is refreshing to encounter a poetic approach to inquiry. Of course, new ways of understanding experience can come from the use of poetry. Likewise, poetry provokes us all to think deeper and to push boundaries. Bochner (2000) calls this approach *poetic social science*. He points out that by using poetry, for example, or any alternative to traditional approaches to research, we add to our knowledge of the social world. In the same way, contemplative research approaches add to our knowledge of the world and of ourselves as researchers. Thus poetry is a solid approach to contemplative inquiry.

The many forms of Japanese poetry are often associated with a Zen mindset. In addition, Chinese poets in the Ch'an, which became Zen tradition, had traditional forms mentioned earlier in this chapter. Many of us are familiar with the pithy, profound, and calming form of Japanese haiku poetry. A haiku poem usually has seventeen syllables in the arrangement of 5/7/5, that is, five syllables, seven syllables, and then five syllables again, and it is usually formatted in three lines. However, this arrangement is not always possible in translations from Japanese to English, so you may see haiku with as few as fifteen syllables or as many as nineteen or twenty. You may also have noticed that Western writers of haiku often vary the style of seventeen syllables. The major focus of haiku is to get to the meaning of the poem with no excess.

There are various other forms of Japanese poetry such as tanka, or sedoka, for example. Still, the main form and the one most often used by Zen teachers is that of haiku. It is very close to Zen, as there are no frills in Zen. The haiku is designed to provoke thought, and thought can lead to self knowledge, which, through meditation, leads to non-self. As pointed out earlier in this book, qualitative researchers may find this thinking helpful. Poetry offers us a way to expand our view of inquiry by including a wide variety of approaches in representing research theory, practice, and findings. We might think about poetry for data presentation and representation and for interpretations of literature in the traditional literature review, themes, and findings. Another place for poetry in a qualitative report would be the concluding sections of the narrative. As well as haiku, two additional approaches for qualitative researchers are *found data poems*, and *identity poems*.

What Are Found Data Poetry and Identity Poetry?

Qualitative researchers are accessing a repertoire of techniques used in data representation, as we capture the lived experience of our participants. Poetry is one of these techniques. The use of found data poems, that is, poetry found in the narrative text of the researcher reflective journal, the interview transcripts, or any site documents used in a given study, offers another way of viewing and presenting data. Identity poetry, also called *I Poetry*, adds to our repertoire of techniques, usually for capturing our own stories as researchers in a given study, although the participants in a study may also create identity poetry and offer yet another data set for analysis and interpretation.

Creating and crafting a narrative with interactivity between researcher, participant, and the poetry itself is a goal of I Poetry. With the prevalence of digital cameras, digital video, and YouTube access, qualitative researchers have the opportunity to create new forms of data representation and analysis through the lens of the poet. The use of selfies, You Tube, and various digital sites offers researchers a new way to disseminate their findings in poetic style. For a riveting example of identity poetry, see www.youtube.com/watch?v=gfexOa8-h44. This clip shows the power of Rachel Rostad's Open Mic poem "Names." YouTube offers qualitative researchers a site for dissemination of the story to be told through poetry.

All in all, poetry is a tried and true research method worthy of consideration for data representation and interpretation. In our digital era, another way that is currently popular for representing data is to perform research through poetry, drama, video, or photography. As pointed out in Chapter 6, students are often digital natives and actually prefer digital formats, so it makes sense to capitalize on this strength in the representation of qualitative research data.

Poetry is popular on the Web. I recently posted the following haiku about meaning.

Meaning comes with solitude
Like the egret on the water
Silence again.

Poetry sutra

Poetry is the journal of the sea animal living on land, wanting to fly in the air. Poetry is the search for syllables to shoot at the barriers of the unknown and the unknowable. Poetry is a phantom script telling how rainbows are made and why they go away.

Carl Sandburg, Poetry Considered, *1923*

Theoretical Frame for Thinking Poetically

The theoretical frame that guides this kind of qualitative work emerges from the work of John Dewey in *Art as Experience* (1934) and from Elliot Eisner's major texts and articles (1981, 1994, 1997, 2004) and may be categorized as interpretive approaches to qualitative research. Conceptually, such interpretive approaches assume that there are multiple ways the world can be known and represented. Knowledge is constructed from experience, and the arts can easily lead to deeper experience of the world. Qualitative inquiry becomes more complete and informative when we increase the range of our description, explanation, and interpretation of the social world. Obviously with new forms of interpretation, new competencies will be required to refine the practice of description, explanation, and interpretation of the social context under study.

There is no end to the number of theoretical frames available for use in the social sciences. For researchers in training, there are a number of solid theoretical frames to learn about and to use as a foundation for their research projects. We are fortunate that, in the social sciences, this theory has received a great deal of study and refinement. A look at the latest dissertations posted on ProQuest in terms of dissertation abstracts shows that the most frequently used theoretical frames in qualitative research projects are social constructionism, phenomenology, and various forms of post structuralism. These methods are fluid, in that they also fit with arts based research approaches.

Found Data Poetry

Found data poetry can be useful in making sense of a transcript, as shown in the following examples.

....

Transcript excerpts, reflections, description
of participants and poetry found in the data

The World Wide Web has numerous oral history transcripts of New York firefighters, police and emergency medical technicians (EMTs) following the 9/11 attacks. These stories can be found at: http://graphics8.nytimes.com/packages/html/nyregion/20050812_ WTC_GRAPHIC/met_WTC_histories_full_01.html

....

At this open access site, the *New York Times* has made available to the public over 500 transcripts that help in understanding the perspectives of the first responders. The site was fought over for five years, but the first responders ultimately triumphed in the court battle that made these transcripts available for all. I use these examples in my classes to illustrate how to create poetry from interview transcripts and/or documents. The following example is taken from the interview of a first responder who is a nurse.

....

Excerpt from a transcript of an interview with EMT
Diane DeMarco, Nurse. Interview date: December 14, 2001.

Q: *Diane, can you tell me what happened that day?*
A: I was assigned to unit 15 Boy, tour 2 that morning. I had responded up to the final outpost to pick up a partner. When I arrived

at the outpost, there was a call given of, I think it's a 1040, plane into building. Shortly after that I was assigned to the job.... I was working with another EMT, Thomas Lopez.... We had gotten to the location of Vesey and West. There was really no one in charge down there. We were basically in charge of ourselves, which worked out pretty well. A supervisor had been passing us by...he directed us into the building, the second floor of the building with our equipment.

I don't know what happened. A couple of minutes after that, I saw my partner get his bags and start towards the building. I told him—I had turned around myself. I had started to go get my tech bag, and I realized this is not a good idea. So I called Tommy back. He came back to the vehicle. And just as he came to the vehicle with me, a couple other units had come down and said, "Let's turn the vehicle around," because we were facing into the location. So myself and a medic unit—I don't know how many other units—turned the vehicles around.

Shortly—I don't know, it would have been minutes, seconds after we turned the vehicle around—the first building fell, the first collapse. At that point there was a car blocking the area, and I was going to attempt to turn that vehicle around. It belonged to a chief that had just passed me by. I knew that he was in front of the hotel. I attempted to walk toward the hotel, but just as I attempted to do that the—I don't know what to call it, the mushroom, avalanche thing—was coming at us. I turned around and called to my partner. We got back in the vehicle and started to pull away from the scene. But just at that point, somebody was pounding on the glass back doors of the ambulance. I looked through the rear view mirror, and I saw a man in a hazmat suit. But I couldn't stop the vehicle because something would have happened to either the vehicle or him. So I sort of motioned to him, but I don't know if he saw me, that I knew he was there on the back bumper of the ambulance. So I drove off, but I drove at a steady pace so that I wouldn't knock him—he wouldn't fall off.

I pulled up a few blocks from there. I don't know what location that was. As I attempted to go around to the back of the vehicle, I saw the man that was on the back of the bumper. He was a sergeant from hazmat, Port Authority. At that point he thanked me. He said that I saved his life because he couldn't run anymore. We then proceeded to treat him, my partner and I. We just did the normal protocol. He was covered in dust. As my partner was treating him, I noticed several fire department personnel, firemen, walking aimlessly or sitting on the corner of where I had pulled in. I don't know the location…so I started to take firemen off the street corners wherever I was finding them. They were totally covered in dust, caked, on their eyelids. So my partner and I again started to treat people…as we were doing that the second tower collapsed. So everybody scattered, and they started running… and we got into the vehicle and started to drive off.… I think that's where I got to Chambers Street, after the second collapse.

In our work as qualitative researchers, one of the surprises is what we may find in any given interview. In this example, the nurse goes to work, like any other day, but what happens that day affects her for life. The immediacy of the description offers food for poetry. See the following example of haiku from this same excerpt.

An ordinary blue sky

An ordinary blue sky
Two buildings collapse
Everything changes.

As mentioned earlier, poetry is a way to present the data in a creative style. In no way does it cast aside the transcript. Instead, it gives renewed life to the transcript. Found data poetry can also be used to capture theory, content, conclusions, and recommendations for future research. To use another example, Slotnick (2010), while analyzing her data for her dissertation, presented a good deal of it in found data poetry. She studied university and community college administrators' perceptions of the transfer process for under-represented students, focusing on three cases of university and community college agreements involving a total of six institutions. Presenting her data for each case, she introduced the participant with a found data poem created from a transcript.
Here is her poem for Bobby.

Bobby

The disadvantages are drastic
In a higher education system not plastic
The inequities are clearly horrific

Especially for the diversity specific
Punitive excess credits will be
For those with career uncertainty
Better academic advising a must
Starting at the community college a plus. (p.130)

Poetry Created from Reflections on Research

The following reflection and poem were inspired by completing a dissertation on the use of technology in education (Stevenson, 2002).

....

Impact of the Study on the Researcher, by Carolyn Stevenson

Journal Excerpt

As a result of this study, I have grown in knowledge and understanding of not only instructional technology but also the leadership needed to bring about institutional and departmental changes. Personally, I have changed my perspective on the roles of educational leaders and technology use. Through completion of this study I have gained a better understanding of the process of change. Through interviewing, observing, and "living" the experiences of the six educational leaders in the study, I was given a unique opportunity to experience their daily activities. It was also an amazing opportunity to learn and grow from their experience. This insight is invaluable as I begin the journey toward pursuing a career in academia.

I have also realized the importance of collaboration, motivation, and teamwork. After reading my journal entries, these elements clearly stood out. Bringing about major changes requires the feedback and advice from everyone in the learning community. Journal writing in itself was an opportunity to reflect on many personal issues. I was able to slow down and reflect upon my experiences during the entire dissertation process. This caused me to analyze the past, live in the present, and plan for the future. I also realized that throughout this process I have grown in ways often difficult to express to others. Journaling provided an outlet for all of the thoughts going on in my head and an opportunity to go back and reflect on the dissertation process.

Research and Reflection, by Carolyn Stevenson

Empowering others to promote change

The researcher is driven by the significance of the work

Passion for the craft lends oneself to fostering individual and
   organizational renewal

Seeking multiple perspectives from which individuals view the world

Purposeful intentions, reflective thought

The researcher experiences the lives of others for only a brief period
   of time

But the impact from meaningful work lasts a lifetime.

Life's Work, by Carolyn Stevenson

Life's work is a journey

Looking into the lives of others

An observer into a lived experience

Research beyond the books

Seeking to describe and explain

Social phenomena that will create positive change

Change in others as well as change in self.

   I offer the preceding examples to guide the reader to see the possibilities in accessing poetry for representing data, for descriptions
of the role of the researcher, and for describing participants, findings, conclusions, reflections, and recommendations.

Identity Poetry

Also known as I Poetry, identity poetry is about getting to your identity
in written verse or any other form of poetry. It can be used to assist
researchers to identify themselves in a poetic idiom. Similarly, in Zen
practice, individuals usually attempt to work toward internal change
through meditation, poetry, and writing a journal to track their progress. One's own history is honored through identity poetry.

   I use a particular guide to help learners get started and begin their
poetic journey. The guide is based on work in class, student input and

rewriting ideas about poetry. Usually, many students say things like, "I cannot write poetry" or "I am not a poet" or other variations of this thinking. However, with this guide they find they can create poetry and go further in their rewriting. I presented the guide at the 10th International Congress on Qualitative Inquiry (ICQI) in Urbana, Illinois, in May 2014 in a session titled "Women who Write." I spoke about writing poetry and got the audience involved in this activity. The audience included graduate students, faculty, researchers from around the globe, and various visitors.

Identity Poetry Activity Prompt

Identity poetry is a good beginning for any poet. Use the following activity prompt to get started on writing identity poetry. It is not meant to encourage slavish adherence to every line. Instead, individuals should pick and choose to find the prompt that inspires their story.

Where I am from

I am from (place of birth)_____

I am from (home adjective)_____

I am from (plant, flower that represents you)_____

I am from (family tradition) _____

I am from the (family tendency) _____

I am from (something you were told as a child)_____

I am from (spiritual tradition) _____

I am from (ethnicity)_____

I am from (stories about) _____

I am from (two food items representing your family) _____

I am from (memories you have) _____

Following this activity at the ICQI session, I asked for volunteers to read their poem and actually had to limit the number of readers. Remarks afterwards indicated the profound effect that speaking their poems had for the volunteers.

For qualitative researchers, I Poetry is a potential tool for coming to grips with the role of the researcher, interpreting the meaning of the findings, and rendering any amount of text poetically. Consider this example by Ruth Slotnick from a recent email exchange. I sent her the prompt to see if it made sense to her, and she emailed me the following poem.

I Am From, by Ruth C. Slotnick

I am from
Pennsylvania,
Amish earth,
A wandering Jew.

I am from,
Small family gatherings
Fraught with psychosis,

It can happen again
In every living thing.

I am from
Sephardic-Ashkenazic,
Latkes and Manischevitz,

Reinventing self
In Yiddish song, opera, arts, and education.

In this fine example, Ruth acknowledges her personal history. As a qualitative researcher herself, she may use something like this in her descriptions of who she sees herself to be.

The next example is a poem that I wrote as part of my own identity poetry, upon completing a seven day yoga workshop. It was written in my yoga journal. The teacher was a master teacher from the Chicago Yoga Center, and I took copious notes before, during, and after classes. After the week of classes I wrote this summary of the week as an example of identity poetry. I also use poetry in my meditation journal as it helps me meditate.

Yoga Rules

Locate your spine, says the teacher,
Energetically push your kidneys into the mat.

Educate your 2nd toe,
Hang around in that pose for some time.

Notice your disorganized thinking,
Activate the interior of your floating ribs.

Let your heart hang humbly forward.

Use the entire periphery of your skin
As you roll from side to side.

Use your skin to bring data to yourself.
Address your right hip

And investigate your breath.

Step into your emotions
And keep your brain cool.

Permit your body to do its natural thing,
Stay for some time in the bones.

Feel your connective tissues
Under the muscles

Breathe into the edges of your diaphragm
Locate your spine.

What poetry teaches me as a student of Zen meditation and yoga, and as a qualitative researcher, is that what we design in research is as closely connected to our bodies as our minds. Furthermore, by the act of writing and recording our history of the experience, we come closer to understanding our place in any research project and certainly in daily life.

Another type of identity poetry is being used by emerging scholars completing research projects such as the dissertation. In the following example, De Felice (2013) writes haiku about the methodology used in his study of endangered languages in Mexico.

A Haiku on my Study

My super study
Surprises, Strengths, Savvy
And Serendipitous.

On Phenomenology

Methodology
It's Phenomenology
Lived experience.

Thus, poetry provides a vehicle to capture many components of any given qualitative study. Found data poems from transcriptions, notes, or the researcher reflective journal provide a way to find a new point of view, and identity poetry offers a way to present thoughts and feelings about qualitative work. Just like Zen practice, writing poetry then becomes a regular and sustained practice.

Poetry as Inquiry

Researchers (Furman, 2006; Willis, 2002) have been suggesting for some time that poetry is a form of inquiry and I agree. Using poetic devices of any kind in the act of writing takes us to another level of thinking, something the ancient writers knew so well. Contrasted with the analytical approach of traditional research, poetic approaches are expressive. They get to the emotional level of arts based inquiry. Denzin (1997) suggests that expressive approaches to research provoke deep and powerful emotions which, in turn, contribute to how we think about data, its visual representation, and its meaning. This is a good reason to use poetry as one of the aesthetic ways to talk about data, talk about your role in a study, and talk about interpretation and meaning.

Summary

Interviews, observations, site documents, photographs, and the researcher reflective journal are the heart and soul of qualitative research. Once these texts are in hand, we then need to make sense of them. Poetry is a useful approach of making sense of data. It provides a way to look at the data in your transcript and render it in poetic form. This chapter presented examples of Zen poetry, and examples of how poetry might be created from interview data and any documents from a study. Poetry forms described included haiku, found data poems, and I Poems, or identity poetry. Poetry provides an aesthetic component to our data as well as a way to make meaning. Creation of found data poems in a format of choice such as haiku, free flow poetry, and any other poetic device allows for ways to include arts-based methods of inquiry in the narrative descriptions of research. Zen teachers have always used poetry; they recommend writing poetry to inform and develop the mind and the ability to meditate. Doing meditation is something like writing poetry, as you need to be deeply focused and engaged to allow for becoming awake to the present moment and all the potential therein.

> Mindful Moment: Sit or lie down for twenty minutes and meditate by being aware of your breathing in and out. As Thich Nhat Hanh suggests, say the words, "Breathing in I calm my feelings, breathing out I smile at my feelings." Now, write in your meditation journal.

Mindful Activities

1. Create one found data poem from a transcript or other document. Next, create one identity poem based on the guide provided earlier and then modify it according to your thinking. Now, find someone who will listen while you read your poems.

2. Meditate on poetry in your life. Write a poetry memory trail. When did you first hear or read poetry? Which poets do you recall and why? When did you write your first poem? Write a few lines about that experience. Write a poem about your current thinking process.

3. Meditate on your right thumb. Move it around a bit. How does it feel? What connections do you notice? Now, bring it back to a still position. Look at the nail of your thumb. Imagine going deeper and relaxing all the veins and muscles of the thumb and hand. Imagine your cells in the thumb. Write in your meditation journal about your thumb.

Suggested Resources for Further Understanding

About Poetry

Oliver, M. (1994). *A poetry handbook*. Orlando, FL: Harcourt Brace.

Eisner, E. W. (1998). *The enlightened eye: Qualitative inquiry and the enhancement of educational practice*. Columbus, OH: Merrill.

Goodman, J. (2011). *Poetry: Tools and techniques*. Vancouver, BC: Gneiss Press.

Tucker, S. (1992). *Writing poetry*. Tucson, AZ: Good Year Books.

About Zen Approaches

Hanh, T. N. (2009). *You are here: Discovering the magic of the present moment*. Boston, MA: Shambala Press.

CHAPTER EIGHT

A Zen Vista of the Researcher Reflective Journal

Whereas the logical mode of thought can only manipulate the world view of a given paradigm, intuition can inspire genuine creativity, since it is not shackled by the nagging analytical mind, which often serves only to intimidate imaginative thought.

Creativity koan

Introduction

The researcher reflective journal is a record of all that is occurring in the study, the processes of the study, and most importantly, the meaning of the study. It is very much like the Zen journals that individuals keep while they are learning to meditate. It may also serve as a space for any notes taken during the actual interviews, afterthoughts, and general impressions of the interview (see Appendix G). Many researchers use art work such as poetry, drawings, or even mini paintings in their journals. A reflective journal kept during a research study may also be used for sections of the final report such as describing the researcher's role as a researcher. The researcher reflective journal is both another data set and a part of final analysis of the project. You might write in the researcher reflective journal about the theory that guides your work or outline alternative explanations for your data. You might also write about the impact of the qualitative research project on you as a qualitative researcher. The following example is a written journal narrative of Stevenson's work (2002) and her growth as a professional, turned researcher.

Valerie J. Janesick, "A Zen Vista of the Researcher Reflective Journal" in *Contemplative Qualitative Inquiry: Practicing the Zen of Research*, pp. 127-140. © 2015 Left Coast Press, Inc. All rights reserved.

....

Journal excerpt on learning to complete my dissertation study
In this excerpt, the researcher/writer takes a contemplative approach to
how she came to finish her dissertation. She has recounted in her earlier journal entries how she worked in factories, in publishing, and now
in teaching immigrants, before coming to her dissertation.

> A valuable concept I learned during my undergraduate years was
> the difference between work and a career. During my freshman and
> sophomore years, I worked in a factory assembling police lights. To
> this day, I do not know which is more arduous: performing tasks that
> were physically exhausting or those that were mentally exhausting.…
> I made it my personal mission to gain teaching experience with the
> hopes of landing a full-time position in higher education. Finally, I
> had found my passion.
>
> My early experiences as a full-time instructor were very Pollyanna
> as I believed that all students wanted to earn a college degree, obtain
> a fulfilling career, and change their lives. It was very disappointing to
> realize that many students lack the desire to graduate from college.
> However, it was inspiring to know that an effective instructor has the
> ability to inspire others and help the dedicated to achieve their dream.
> During my first year teaching full-time I also gave birth to my daugh-
> ter. I continued working full-time until I made the decision to return
> to school to pursue a doctoral degree in educational leadership and
> organizational change.
>
> During my doctoral studies I had the opportunity to gain first-
> hand experience with working with the elementary schools. I de-
> signed, managed, and obtained funding for a parent-child literacy
> program that involved working with a probationary school on Chi-
> cago's South Side. It was a real eye-opener to experience the struggles
> of many lower-income families. Despite heroic efforts by the school
> administration and staff, there is no way to control the environment a
> child is raised in. A few blocks outside the "safe school zone" revealed
> urban warfare and tales of children being shuffled from one caregiv-
> er to the next. However, working with the program allowed me to
> assist parents and children and one small hug from a child or word of
> thanks from a parent speak volumes. Fortunately I was able to identify
> a career I have true passion for: higher education. With this determi-
> nation I set forth on my journey. Despite personal problems, I was the
> first in my cohort to successfully defend my dissertation. I wrote every

day and despite handling many responsibilities, I became consumed with my writing. The demands of a qualitative dissertation are intense; and I often wondered where I drew my inner strength to persevere. After perusing through my reflective journal kept while writing the dissertation, I came across the following entry, the first written in a daily ritual.

September, 2001

After recently hearing a speech from a graduate, I felt a wake-up call to the enormous task ahead. However, organization and commitment will get you through… I think my major roadblock is deciding on a topic. Once my focus is clear, the live-breath dissertation process begins. The classroom presentation re-emphasized the importance of organization, dedication, and self-discipline needed to finish the dissertation. Fortunately, I still follow the advice I received in a class taken the first quarter: Do something every day. That's critical, involves sacrifice but keeps you on top of things. I realized that qualitative research would get to stories of real people. I also enjoy the interviewing process and learning about others' life experience. So the process though it involves much more work than crunching numbers from a random survey, seems enjoyable.

In a first attempt to begin the dissertation process, I "cleaned house" and organized old research papers, notes, books, and cleared out file cabinets. I also reread parts of various texts which makes so much more sense to me now than the first read. Although I knew I had anxiety about the dissertation, the chapter helped me recognize these thoughts are completely normal. Most importantly, self-confidence is so, so important. Now is not the time to question writing ability or dedication. Focus and confidence are needed. So, at the present, I have a long way to go in this saga. I truly enjoy writing and researching so once I begin, I will not stop. There is so much I need to learn about qualitative research. The rest lies in my hands.…

Completing the dissertation was by far, the single greatest challenge I have ever faced. Perhaps the impact the study had on me can best be expressed from an excerpt from my dissertation.

As a result of this study, I have grown in knowledge and understanding of not only instructional technology, but also the leadership needed to bring about institutional and departmental changes. For me, I have changed my perspective on the roles of educational leaders and technology use. Prior to this study, I was unaware of the varied nature and responsibilities held by the educational leaders of various levels. I discovered that deans have a genuine interest in student and curriculum concerns. I have also gained a better understanding of the process of change, in particular the steps and challenges involved with incorporating instructional technology use into the curriculum. Through interviewing, observing, and "living" the experiences of the six educational leaders, I was given a unique opportunity to experience their daily activities. It was also an amazing opportunity to learn from their experience. This insight is invaluable as I begin the journey toward pursuing a career in academia.

I have also realized the importance of collaboration, motivation, and teamwork. After reading my journal entries, these elements clearly stood out. Bringing about major changes requires the feedback and advice from everyone in the learning community. Journal writing in itself was an opportunity to reflect on many personal issues. I was able to slow down and reflect upon my experiences during the entire dissertation process. This caused me to analyze the past, live in the present, and plan for the future. I also realized that throughout this process I have grown in ways often difficult to express to others. Journaling provided an outlet for all of the thoughts going on in my head and an opportunity to go back and reflect on the dissertation process and on self. This study also enabled me to focus on a future career path. I have always enjoyed technology and learning about ways it can improve my life. It was enjoyable talking to others about their experiences with technology. From the participants, I realized that I enjoy the administrator's role and taking on new challenges. I was amazed at the amount of change the two educational leaders were able to accomplish in a relatively short period of time. In an environment that was not conducive to change, they broke the barriers and made change happen. After reflecting upon women's roles in higher education, I decided that I would not sell out and take on yet another "job." I realized that I need to find a rewarding and challenging career in my field.

Fortunately and in retrospect, I was able to find a position as an Assistant Professor of English & Communications at a small private four-year college. My experience pursuing a doctorate in Educational Leadership and Organizational Change awoke the leader within. Since my interests lie in both areas, I have flexibility with course assignments and teach both English and Communications courses. I found my path.

In the preceding example, we have a section of the story of an individual's lived experience through the individual's words written as reflective journal text. This text adds to the record of the study and to the record of women's lives so often missing in traditional approaches and so often forgotten. Journal writing is a powerful tool for practicing writing, like the practice of Zen meditation. One learns to write by writing. One learns to meditate by meditating.

Mindful Moment: Keep a researcher reflective journal and a meditation journal. Record your impressions, thoughts, beliefs, and any challenges in each process. Note changes and growth. Get into the habit of writing and rewriting.

Journal Writing as a Contemplative Research Technique

I have been writing about the researcher reflective journal since the 1990s and see now that the written and published works today about journal writing are expanding. In terms of this book, a reflective journal may be considered a contemplative research technique in qualitative studies. It is contemplative as a result of the time spent on meditating or thinking about the meaning of the data in any given study. It also helps the researcher slow down. For qualitative researchers, the act of journal writing, incorporated into the research process, can provide a data set of the researcher's reflections on the research act, beginning to end, as well as on the story being told. Participants in qualitative studies may also use journals to refine ideas, beliefs, and their responses to the research in progress. Finally, sharing journal writing between participants and researcher may offer the qualitative researcher yet another opportunity for triangulation of data sets at multiple levels.

Journal writing has a long and reliable history in the arts and humanities, and qualitative researchers may learn a great deal from this record. It is not by accident that artists, writers, musicians, dancers, therapists, physicians, poets, architects, saints, chefs, scientists, and educators use journal writing in their lives. In virtually every field, one can find exemplars who have kept detailed and lengthy journals regarding their everyday lives and their beliefs, hopes, and dreams. I see journal writing as a powerful heuristic tool and research technique that can be useful in qualitative research projects for the following reasons:

1. to refine and define the understanding of the role of the researcher in the study;
2. to refine the understanding of the responses of the participants;
3. as a means to communicate with participants and for them to communicate with the researcher;
4. for researchers to become more contemplative and reflect on their own thinking;
5. for researchers to grow and develop capacity as a researcher; and
6. for enjoyment of writing, for a creative outlet, and for gaining understanding.

The notion of a comprehensive reflective journal to address the researcher's self is critical in qualitative work due to the fact that the researcher is the *research instrument*. A review of the literature in this area shows that journal writing, although an ancient technique, is only now being used and talked about as a serious component in qualitative research projects. I have always seen journal writing as a major source of data. It is a data set that contains the researcher's reflection on the role of the researcher, for example, providing a vehicle for coming to terms with exactly what one is doing as the qualitative researcher. As well, it is a good place to record the twists and turns taken in a study, for example, when a participant mentions something unexpected in an interview and completely changes the focus of the interview.

Qualitative researchers are often criticized for not being precise about what they do. I offer journal writing as a technique to accomplish the description and explanation of the researcher's role in the project. In addition, participants in a project often find a journal helpful for remembering experiences that connect to their present story. In every research project I am involved with as researcher/interviewer, I give notebooks to the participants to jot down things they recall after their interviews. For example, I have recently been conducting oral history interviews with women leaders and have given each of them a notebook. I also carry one to jot down ideas I need to develop in any of my work. Alternately, I carry my IPad everywhere and use the Notes application as my journal. I also use www.penzu.com, a website that offers a free, open access, online journal just for you once you set up an account. It has unlimited storage and is useful for keeping your journal in digital format.

> *Journal writing sutra:* whether you're keeping a journal or writing as a meditation, it's the same thing. What's important is that you are having a relationship with your mind.
>
> *Natalie Goldberg (2005)*

Writing about Challenges in a Study

Qualitative researchers can also use a reflective journal to write about the problems that come up in a study, often on a regular basis. Such problems involve things like the representation of interviews and field notes, transcripts, translations when participants use another language, co-construction of meaning with participants in the project who also keep a journal, and the interpretation of each other's data. Deciding what goes into the narrative and what is left out can be difficult. Ethical issues are also bound to emerge from time to time in any study, and can be described and explained in the journal. By reflecting on these issues and journaling one's thoughts, one can more easily write a rationale for deciding which of them will be left in and which will be left out. As researchers, we often are positioned outside the very people and situations we write about. Journal writing personalizes representation in a way that forces the researcher to confront the issue of how a story from a person's life becomes a public text, which in turn tells a story. How else are we to make sense of the lived experience of the participants?

Journal writers across many disciplines have weighed in on this subject. For example, therapists view the journal as an attempt to bring order to one's experience and a sense of coherence to one's life. Behaviorists, cognitivists, and Jungian analysts use journals in the process of therapy. The journal is seen as a natural outgrowth of the clinical situation in which the client speaks to the self. Most profoundly, Ira Progoff (1992) has written about using an intensive journal. Progoff developed a set of techniques that provide a structure for keeping a journal and a springboard for development. As a therapist, he conducted workshops and trained a network of individuals to do workshops on keeping an intensive journal to unlock one's creativity and come to terms with one's self. The intensive journal method is a reflective, in-depth process of writing, speaking what is written, and in some cases sharing what is written with others. Feedback is an operative principle for the Progoff method. The individual needs to draw upon inner resources to arrive at the understanding of the whole person; the journal is a tool to reopen the possibilities of learning and living. Progoff advocated the following:

1. regular entries in the journal in the form of dialogue with one's self,

2. maintaining the journal as an intensive psychological workbook in order to record all encounters of one's existence, and

3. some type of sharing of this growth through journal writing with others.

The Progoff method makes use of a special bound notebook divided into finite categories that include: dreams, stepping stones, and dialogues with persons, events, work, and the body. The writer is asked to reflect, free associate, meditate, and imagine that which relates to immediate experience. The latest version of Progoff's text (1992) is a strong testimonial to the method and provides useful examples of techniques for keeping a journal. There is also a website entirely devoted to Ira Progoff's latest versions of the Intensive Journal Workshop, and it is a jewel of a resource on journal writing. Obviously, anyone can write a journal without this structure. However, the value of the structure is that it forces reflection, recollection and, usually, growth. Zen practitioners also use journal writing to chart their thoughts, values, beliefs, and progress toward refining their meditation practice and life as it is lived. Every one of my meditation teachers keeps a journal, as do I. The journal also prompts regular writing. For those of us who do writing for a living, it is a tested and true technique.

Journal writing is so prevalent now that one only has to surf the Internet to see thousands of journal resources, examples, and personal histories online. There is an online course on journal writing offered by

Via Creativa, chat rooms on journal writing, exemplars of diaries and journal writing, and literally thousands of similar resources. You may be somewhat overwhelmed by the multitude of sources. As with anything on the Internet, you will have to sift through these resources to see what is best for your learning style. In general, the common thread that unites them all is the theme that journal writing is a way of getting in touch with yourself in terms of reflection, catharsis, remembrance, creation, exploration and problem solving, problem posing, and personal growth. All of these habits improve the act and the art of interviewing. Practiced routinely, journal writing itself becomes a habit and thus assists in the work we do as qualitative researchers.

While journal writing has its seeds in psychology, sociology, and history, I rely on social psychology for understanding the use of the journal. Basically, the practice of journal writing and subsequent interpretation of journal writing produce meaning and understanding that are shaped by genre, the narrative form used, and the personal cultural and paradigmatic conventions of the writer, who is the researcher, participant, and/or co-researcher. As Progoff (1992) notes, journal writing is ultimately a way of getting feedback from ourselves. In so doing, it enables us to experience, in a full and open-ended way, the movement of our lives as a whole and the meaning that follows from reflecting on that movement. Journal writing is a contemplative act. It allows one to reflect, to dig deeper into the heart of the beliefs and behaviors described in one's journal. The clarity of writing down one's thoughts allows for stepping into one's inner mind and reaching further into interpretations of the words that one has written. To develop the habit of mind of journal writing, it is a good idea to write every day at a set time. It is also a good idea to meditate every day at the same time. This is Zen in motion. Over time, the habit of journal writing will assist in the eventual construction of the narrative. Writing is always part of contemplation in our work as qualitative researchers.

It also makes sense to cross disciplinary borders so as to integrate poetry, drawing, or photographs, for example, into a journal, a practice that ultimately contributes to the final research narrative. A good strategy in terms of writing is to keep your poems, drawings, sketches or photographs in your researcher reflective journal. By writing reflections on these various items in your journal you clarify your position and situate yourself in the research process. These items fill out the context of the story. Writing about them can work to sharpen your contemplative practices in research. To become a solid writer, it makes sense to write as regularly as you meditate.

To some extent, the use of the reflective journal as part of the data collection procedure supports the credibility and trustworthiness of this technique. It also acts as a source of credibility and descriptive substance for the overall project. As a research technique, keeping a journal with poetry and any other art form is user friendly, meaning that it often instills a sense of confidence in beginning researchers and a sense of accomplishment in experienced researchers. In keeping a journal it is always useful to supply all the basic descriptive data in each entry. Information such as the date, time, place, participants and any other descriptive information should be recorded in order to provide accuracy in reporting later in the study. Especially in long-term projects, specific evidence that locates members and activities can be useful in the final analysis and interpretation of the research findings. Journal writing has an elegant and documented history. Think of yourself as contributing to a long line of historical journal writers.

A Brief History of Journal Writing

We come from a long ancestral line of writers. Throughout history, journal writing has developed as a powerful tool, in a similar fashion to the long line of meditation teachers in Zen and the long line of writers in the field of qualitative research methods. Some of the earliest journals were kept in Greek and Roman times. Later, theologians kept journals as evidenced by the journals of St. Augustine. In Japan, in the 10th century, Japanese "pillow diaries" were regularly used by women in the court who were part of the palace culture and structure. They hid their diaries under their pillows, but they were a way of having a record of their lives and a voice. They recorded hopes, dreams, experiences, feelings, fantasies, and innermost thoughts. Next in history, the Renaissance ushered in an era when many participated in journal writing and when, in fact, journals were read aloud and shared in public and private gatherings. At the time, it was understood that the rebirth of society should be chronicled apart from the heavy handedness of the clergy, and should be described fully and left as a historical record of an exciting era.

Perhaps the most famous was the diary in the 1660s of Samuel Pepys, who, every day for nine years, described nearly every corner of London's daily life. In astonishing detail, he described food, people, politics, the arts, crime, politics, and people's joys and sorrows. Most noteworthy are his descriptions of the monarchy and its transgressions. His thick description of the problems arising from the practices of the Church of England, the navy, in which he served, and the events of the day are, even today, something of an official record. He wrote of the wars and conflicts of his time, the great fire of London, and the plague and its aftermath, yet it took nearly 200 years for his diary to be published, as it did not appear in print until 1825 (Latham & Matthews 1970). The practice took hold, however, and Victorians subsequently focused on letter writing and journals. What is amazing to me, as I look at Pepys' diary, is that many of the same problems of his time are front and center in today's news and popular culture, namely, political conflict, plague, and environmental issues.

Later, organized religious groups such as the Quakers also kept journals. John Wesley, the founder of Methodism, kept volumes of journals. The Puritans were also avid journal writers and record keepers, for example, keeping a meticulous record of the voyage of the Mayflower and their subsequent daily lives in the New World. For people exploring new parts of the globe, the journal was the perfect outlet for recording fears, homesickness, moments of despair, and moments of discovery and joy. Recall that, in those times, communication among individuals and groups was spotty at best. The digital world did not exist, there were no no pagers, no telephones, not even a pony express. Where else could one keep this record? In France, especially during the French Revolution, *journaux intime* were kept to record the personal comments of disgust for the monarchy or of passion for liberty, equality, and fraternity. In the Americas, the diaries of Lewis and Clark, the slave narratives, and other historical accounts come to us from the act of journal writing.

Journal writing began from a need to tell a story, to collect one's thoughts, and to keep a historical record and embellish it with poetry, drawing, or any other art form. Famous journal writers throughout history have provided us with eminent examples of various categories and types of journals. Progoff (1992), for example once again, suggests using a dialogue journal where, as writers, you and I would imagine a dialogue going on among ourselves, our bodies, our friends, and society. In this format, one actually writes the dialogue, posing thoughtful questions and providing answers. No matter what orientation is taken by the journal writer, it is generally agreed that reflective journal writing is undertaken for attaining crispness of description and meaning, organizing one's thoughts and feelings, and, eventually, achieving understanding. Thus, the qualitative researcher has a valuable tool in reflective journal writing. In a sense, the journal writer is interacting with his or her own thinking.

The practice of journal writing and subsequent interpretations of journal writing produce meaning and understanding that are shaped by genre, the particular narrative form used, and personal cultural and paradigmatic conventions of the writer, who may be the researcher, participant, or co-researcher. In doing this type of writing, we develop a routine that can become our most useful habit in our daily work as a qualitative researcher. Journal writing allows us to reflect, to become more contemplative in whatever terms we describe our journals. The act of writing down our thoughts allows us to step into our inner mind and extend our reach for clarity in the interpretation of the behaviors and beliefs expressed in the words that we write. Ultimately, the journal becomes a tool for training us in our role as research instrument. Since qualitative social science relies heavily on the researcher as the research instrument, journal writing can only assist researchers in reaching their goal in any given project. I see journal writing as a critical tool in the process of becoming a solid narrative writer, a proficient qualitative researcher, and a developing poet.

Poetry, journal writing, and, indeed, all writing that we do can become transdisciplinary, that is, it can be used in at least two disciplines, and thus can enrich our final narrative. By using arts-based approaches that work in a transdisciplinary way, we also come closer to a social justice approach to research by virtue of the inclusive nature of the work. For one thing, many researchers find ways to keep a journal and write poetry. As the records show, some information that is gathered and shared in qualitative work is basically private, that is, the participant would like to keep it private, and so any video and audio materials need to be protected just as the hard text in a research report is considered confidential and is protected. In other words, ethical principles form an overriding umbrella for researchers in terms our work. At the same time, with the proliferation of social media, YouTube, and other readily available technology, the current generation of researchers seems dedicated to, if not glued to, computers and hand held devices that basically open up a world that previously might have been private. There will always be discussion on balancing the private and the public; I have found that the best way to approach this discussion is openly, in dialogue, and with the goal of coming to a reasonable solution for all parties. Writing down thoughts such as these helps to keep the historical record in place and also serves to develop our writing abilities.

Technology is, indeed, a welcome addition to the tool kit of the journal writer/researcher (see Appendices D and F). Through technology we now have a way to store our journals digitally and disseminate our work instantly. Using technology starts with the basics, as discussed earlier, and then developmentally figuring out a way to tell someone's story in photographs, video, poetry, visual text, etc. Some researchers also use social networks such as Facebook or Twitter, blogs, wikis, YouTube, and TeacherTube to collect data and represent the data through technology, which essentially is a move to go beyond the one-dimensional interview transcript and make full use of its content. Through YouTube alone, technology has assisted in the dissemination of spoken-word data such as identity poetry. Any of the national poetry slams found on YouTube offer an excellent example of how the spoken word is often as powerful as written text. YouTube is a perfect vehicle for experiencing life as it happens. Performance is another way to represent data effectively, and performing some portion of the research reflective journal can be particularly valuable. Through the performance of sections of your reflective journal, you are interpreting the data collected for your study in both a written format and a performance format, thus opening up new ways of thinking about a given event.

Summary

This chapter reviewed major points about the value and uses of the researcher reflective journal. A brief history of the very long history of journal writing was provided. Keeping a research reflective journal is a creative contemplative act related to another good habit, namely, journal writing. Just as Zen teachers advise keeping a meditation journal, we as qualitative researchers can benefit from this ancient technique of keeping a historical record of our work through journaling.

Mindful Activities

1. Write three pages in your journal in the format of a dialogue with

yourself, and write about what you wish to learn from your project.

2. Write three pages in your journal about what you learned about yourself as a researcher, writer, and/or poet.

3. Write one paragraph to describe yourself as a contemplative writer.

4. Write a short poem in any style about your writing style and content.

5. Design a cover for your researcher reflective journal and one for your meditation journal.

Suggested Resources for Further Understanding

Books and Journal Articles

Glesne, C. (1997). That rare feeling: Re-presenting research through poetic transcription. *Qualitative Inquiry, 3,* 202-221.

Janesick, V. J. (1999). A journal about journal writing as a qualitative research technique: History, issues, and reflections. *Qualitative Inquiry, 5,* 505-524.

Mallon, T. (1995). *A book of one's own: People and their diaries.* St. Paul, MN: Hungry Mind Press.

Nin, A. (1976). *The diary of Anais Nin 1955-1966.* G. Stuhlman (Ed.). New York: Harcourt, Brace.

Pepys, S. (2003). *The diary of Samuel Pepy.* R. Gallienne (Ed.). Modern Library Paperback Edition. New York: Random House.

Progoff, I. (1992). *At a journal workshop: Writing to access the power of the unconscious and evoke creative ability.* Los Angeles: Jeremy P. Tarcher, Inc.

Rainer, T. (1978). The new diary. New York: G. P. Putnam.

Slotnick, R. & Janesick, V. J. (2011). Conversations on method: Deconstructing policy through the researcher reflective journal. *The Qualitative Report, 16*(5), 1352-1360. Retrieved from www.nova.edu/ssss/QR/QR16-5?slotnick.pdf

Web Resources

intensivejournal.org/index.php

This is the site for Progoff's intensive journal writing method. He suggests writing in a dialogue format and getting feedback.

 **CHAPTER NINE**

Satori, Zenergy, and Understanding

A monk told Joshu, "I have just entered the monastery. Please teach me." Joshu asked, "Have you eaten your rice porridge?" The monk replied, "I have eaten." Joshu said, "Then you had better wash your bowl." At that moment the monk was enlightened.

Wash your Bowl koan

Understanding Satori

Satori is the Japanese Buddhist word for understanding and enlightenment. The great Zen teacher Suzuki (2011) said that it means acquiring a new point of view in our dealings with life, and I agree. For those of us who practice qualitative research techniques it certainly has resonance, as we strive to describe and explain the perspectives of our participants' experiences and their meaning. In addition, satori might refer to our own attempts to come to understanding in our work. We need to be able to describe our role in any given research project in detail and thoroughly, which demands that we know ourselves, our place in the research project, and our contemplative practice in the form of thinking, writing, and rewriting. Finally, we need satori to be able to tell the story. In a sense, satori includes being able to see the world from the participant's point of view and the ability to illuminate our understanding of that point of view. Since our body is our research instrument, so to speak, we must endeavor to "get into good shape" with observation, interviewing, writing, reflection, and creativity. You might say we are "working out these muscles"

Valerie J. Janesick, "Satori, Zenergy, and Understanding" in *Contemplative Qualitative Inquiry: Practicing the Zen of Research*, pp. 141-151. © 2015 Left Coast Press, Inc. All rights reserved.

and developing good habits of mind at the same time. Zen offers a way of looking at the world that allows working out these muscles of the qualitative researcher and thus leads to understanding a new point of view. Zen also positions us to slow down and hear the data, write about it in a contemplative way, and share our understandings.

Zenergy, Intuition, and Qualitative Analysis

> Zen is the enemy of analysis, the friend of intuition. The Zen artist understands the ends of art, intuitively, and the last thing s/he would do is to create categories; the avowed purpose of Zen is to eliminate categories! The true Zen-person holds to the Toaist proverb, Those who know, do not speak. Those who speak, do not know.
>
> *Thomas Hoover,* The Zen Experience, *1980*

The issue of analysis presents a problem for someone who is a Zen artist. If one is truly in the Zen mindset, how is one supposed to analyze interviews, the researcher reflective journal entries, photographs, site documents, archives, or any poetry, for example? If Hoover (1980) is correct, categories would, indeed, be the last thing to consider, although they would not be the only thing we are concerned with as qualitative researchers. Nonetheless, as researchers we have to make some meaning of what we are researching. Data do not speak for themselves. Zen produces energy of the mind that I call zenergy. If we can develop this energy of the mind, zenergy, we can make sense of what is before us in the data sets for a given contemplative qualitative inquiry. Furthermore, as mentioned earlier in this book, deepening your intuition is an amazing side effect of meditation. It allows for creativity to awaken and develop.

Zenergy as a Type of Analysis

Qualitative researchers have worked diligently to counter the common misconception that, in qualitative research, anything goes. As a result we have many fine analytical guidelines and textbooks to testify to that effect. Nearly every qualitative research methods text contains suggestions for approaching analysis (see Creswell, 2013; Janesick, 2011;

Lichtmann, 2012; Rubin & Rubin, 2012; Saldana, 2010). In this book, I take a Zen perspective to build up zenergy and to reiterate that understanding is the goal of qualitative researchers. This perspective does not require inventing a new wheel. As in all things Zen, the universe is the space for understanding what is already before you. Our job is to find what is squarely in front of our eyes.

For example, we use induction, deduction, abduction, evaluation, critical thinking, and synthesis on a regular basis. As a result, we can certainly think about which approaches to analysis make sense for a given study. In general, there is agreement that one possibility is to do what best suits the objective of the study. The following list illustrates the complexity of this task. It is not meant to be exhaustive.

Some Qualitative Approaches

Portraiture	Ethnography	Life History
Oral History	Autoethnography	Biography
Case Study	Action Research	Grounded Theory
Historiography	Netnography	Narrative Research

Regardless of what approach is used to do research, there is general agreement on processes. We work constantly with narrative data in the form of interview transcripts and various site documents that might include a resume or curriculum vitae, a syllabus, a written policy, a photograph, a blog entry, a researcher reflective journal entry, etc. Regardless of the text before us, we agree on the general approaches to understanding our data.

Making Your Way to Satori through Analysis

Qualitative researchers often tap into their creativity to make sense of the data collected in a project. Just as we have baby steps in coming into meditation as a practice for life, so too do we take baby steps toward analysis and understanding to reach satori. The following are some of these steps.

1. *Immerse yourself in your data.*

   Get to know your data through and through. After you transcribe your interviews, listen to the data as you read your transcripts. Take notes as you go through this process.

2. *Write in your reflective journal.*

   When you see something that doesn't fit, write about it. Pour through this written work every day. As qualitative researchers we get into the habit of listening to and hearing the data. Likewise, we get into the habit of reading, rereading, writing, and rewriting.

3. *Find your focus.*

   As you sift through the data, you will see certain words and phrases that stick out. Go back to your purpose of the study. Go back to your questions that guide the study. See what is before you. Review the well tested approach to data analysis from Rubin and Rubin (2005, 2013).

Action	Purpose
Recognize	Find the concepts, topics, words in the interviews, or documents.
Examine	Clarify what is meant by these concepts and topics. Synthesize in order to form a narrative.
Code or Name	Find a label or signifier to designate these concepts, topics, etc. Then, rename families of the concepts and topics.
Sort	Group them once again and sift through them to find nuance and overall unity.
Synthesize	Put the concepts, topics, and identifiers into themes and connect these to your research questions.

Another approach to making sense of data is that of Saldana (2013), who advised the researcher to create an initial set of codes; to examine the set for families, which then become categories; and then to look at the categories for families, which then become themes. This, in a nutshell, is the basic thematic analysis that most of us have used.

Another fine example is Visedo's (2012) explanation of her data analysis process. She studied bi-literacy of Spanish/English speakers and their personal histories in education. She devised the following system for her study, combining the principles of Rubin and Rubin, and of Saldana.

Action	Steps
Data Collection	Autobiographies online through blogs, e journals, artifacts, electronic portfolios, and interviews online
Analysis	Total immersion in the data, meticulous reading of texts
	Organizing data into emerging patterns
	Data coding by highlighting, color coding, and comments
	Audits by a critical friend
	Finding patterns, identifying themes
Triangulation	Member checks, negative theme analysis, final themes
Praxis	Find the meaning in the study

In each of these three approaches to data analysis and interpretation we find common activities, which include the following.

- *Finding the codes, categories and themes*

An important thing to recall is that there is no one correct way to do qualitative analysis. These three examples of approaches to analysis are helpful for any qualitative researcher. The Visedo example (2013) is timely since she used technology throughout her study and used Skype interviewing as a key data collection technique. As well, she downloaded and transcribed the interviews with the updated software now available. Once you immerse yourself in the data and find your focus, the codes, categories, and themes emerge organically. Put time into this and it will get you to the interpretation stage.

- *Interpreting your study*

  By using a contemplative approach to inquiry, that is, developing the mind energy that I call zenergy and accessing your creativity and intuition, you are ready to make sense of the data in front of you. In other words, you will have the power to decide which approach to analysis makes sense for your study. Presumably, you already have immersed yourself in the content knowledge and research in your discipline. So, too, you will have immersed yourself in the content area of qualitative research and have conducted a pilot study. So you are now ready to begin making sense of your data in all its forms.

I made a statement earlier in this chapter about Zen being the enemy of analysis, especially when analysis is reduced to simply coding data. Of course, that type of approach has not served us well. However, with a careful connection to the texts of the study, including using your creative mind, spending ample time, and having members of the study doing serious member checking, we move closer to satori. By this I mean that we start seeing ordinary things in a new and extraordinary way. Thus, once you decide which approach to analysis suits your study, following the standard checks and balances in that method is a wise way to proceed.

Checks and Balances in Qualitative Research Methods

Historically speaking, qualitative research methods have been practiced and tested since the first cave paintings in what is now Australia. From pictures that tell a story, to the oral tradition of storytelling, and then to the written word, researchers and storytellers crafted ways to help us to know about the lived experience of a person or group. Letters, diaries, tapestries, paintings, photographs, and manuscripts have long been available and are the beginnings of what we do as qualitative researchers. In the last two centuries, anthropologists, sociologists, and historians took the lead in crafting this field. Now, however, qualitative researchers have more books, articles, journals, listservs, job postings, and YouTube videos on qualitative research methods than in any other time period.

Built into our work is a trustworthy system of checks and balances, or rules of thumb, that assist us in our work. Those rules of thumb include but are not limited to the following.

1. Include a description of your role as the researcher in your final report.

2. Have an outsider peer-review your field notes, observations, interview transcripts, documents, etc. Some writers call this engaging a critical friend, and others call it auditing. The purpose is to have someone else see if your report follows from your data. You may be so close to the data that you miss something obvious. Let an outside reviewer be part of this process.

3. Stay over time. There is no easy way to do this work and it cannot be rushed. To get to a saturation point in terms of meaning, it has always been valuable to stay over a reasonable time period. In our hurried lives there is often a tendency to finish things up quickly. Resist that at all costs. How else can we describe the context of study, let alone capture the lived experience of participants?

4. Have your participants check the data and the interpretations that you make. We call this member checking and it is meant to assist with analysis and interpretation. It enhances the trustworthiness and credibility of the study.

5. Be clear about ethical issues that emerge in the study. Since we are dealing with real people in real settings, there is always bound to be conflict. Problems of one sort or another are always occurring. As ethical issues arise, be straightforward in describing them and how they are resolved.

6. Sift through your data continually and look for statements and assertions by your participants. As you see certain data appearing frequently over time and in more than one interview, you will know you are on the right track as you move toward satori and a new way to look at ordinary data.

7. Slow down. This Zen principle is a good fit for qualitative researchers. Avoid rushing interviews, rushing the analysis, and adding clutter to the mind. Tap into your zenergy.

8. Avoid delusional thinking. There is no need to be deluded by the design or the process of completing a qualitative research project.

These checks and balances assist us in the analysis process.

Why Contemplative Inquiry and the Zen Metaphor?

One of the main reasons I use Zen as a metaphor in contemplative inquiry is that it is particularly well suited to qualitative research methods both in a general, comprehensive way and in many specific ways. The connection to contemplation is straightforward. Nevertheless, in my own experience as a teacher of qualitative research methods for well over three decades and at various universities, qualitative research methods have been looked on as something new or something to be avoided. Zen principles have been around for a very long time, indeed, for centuries, and so there is no need to avoid concepts such as compassion, anti-oppressive pedagogy, impermanence, non-self, or nirvana. As an initiator of qualitative research methods courses in many of the institutions where I served as a faculty member, I was happy to write the course proposals, move them through the various levels of approval, and see the historical record evolve. At the same time, my own study of yoga and meditation developed, and it made sense to connect these two arenas. As qualitative researchers, we strive to do no harm, just like the Zen practitioner. In addition, Zen offers a way to unleash creativity, consciousness, and compassion.

In this book, you have read about using creativity in terms of observation, interviewing, writing up the final story, presenting data, and using poetry and other art forms, all with an eye to ethics. The ethical component in terms of doing no harm is the connection between Zen compassion and contemplative qualitative inquiry. Overarching in both is the consciousness of the three organizing principles of impermanence, non-self, and nirvana.

The following eight well known segments of the path in Zen Buddhism resonate with what we do as qualitative researchers.

Zen Principle	Qualitative Research Principle
Right view	Finding your theoretical frame
Right intention	Daily practice of writing
Right speech	Writing, rewriting
Right action	Writing, rewriting
Right livelihood	Writing, rewriting, insight
Right effort	Analysis, interpretation, meaning
Right mindfulness	Telling the story, insight
Right concentration	Enlightenment, awareness, insight

One of my meditation teachers often speaks of the lessons of his teachers and their teachers and so on back to the Zen tradition of his ancestral line. He regularly mentions understanding the mind. The following lesson is from the words of a great teacher, Yasutani-Roshi, as found in Kapleau (2000). It is about understanding the mind more fully. Zen, more than anything, keeps you in touch with your mind.

Student A (Female, sixty years old, Westerner)

The student asks about the purpose of meditation.

Roshi responds as follows:

> Let us speak of mind first. Your mind can be compared to a mirror which reflects everything that appears before it. From the time you begin to think, to feel, and to exert your will, shadows are cast upon your mind which distort its reflections. This condition we call delusion, which is the fundamental sickness of human beings. The most serious effect of this sickness is that it creates a sense of duality, inconsequence of which you postulate "I" and "not I". The truth is everything is one.... Falsely seeing oneself confronted by a

world of separate existences, this is what creates antagonism, greed, and invariably suffering. The purpose of Zazen (meditation) is to wipe away from the mind these shadows or defilements (delusions) so that we can intimately experience our solidarity with all of life. Love and compassion then naturally and spontaneously flow forth.

What does this lesson mean for the qualitative researcher? Since qualitative researchers, in most cases, are seeking to describe and explain the perspectives of their participants, being more contemplative and acknowledging the solidarity with all of life is a good way to assist in that process. To be truly open to hearing the data in interviews and truly calm in writing and rewriting is a goal that is well worth working toward. Contemplative qualitative inquiry is an idea whose time has come. Zen offers a fitting metaphor for becoming contemplative qualitative researchers.

> Only in an open, nonjudgmental space can we acknowledge what we are feeling. Only in an open space where we are not caught up in our own version of reality can we see and hear and feel who others really are, which allows us to be with them and communicate with them properly.
>
> *Communications sutra, Pema Chodron (2000)*

Summary

This book evolved from a lifetime of qualitative research projects, as well as through studying meditation and yoga. Three key elements of Zen—the concepts of observations being impermanent, interviewing as non-self, and writing as nirvana—are helpful in explaining contemplative qualitative inquiry. Through the use of koans and sutras, mindful activities, and suggestions for further understanding, the intention of the book is to allow the reader to experience Zen, even if at a very basic level. Recommending poetry and journal writing as tools for becoming more contemplative was a secondary intention of this book. Satori, the Japanese Buddhist word for understanding, represents a summary of these possibilities. To slow down, as the Zen teacher advises, can only help us do better at our craft. Using Zen as a metaphor to conduct contemplative qualitative inquiry is a new way of looking at our work, our thinking, and our continuing historical record. As we strive for a more compassionate and humane qualitative research methodology, we can become more Zen-like and more contemplative. This is contemplative qualitative inquiry.

Mindful Activities

1. Create a koan about your qualitative research project and share it with someone for feedback.
2. Create a timeline of your development as a qualitative researcher. Chart your progress to the present. Now, write three pages about your evolution as a researcher and select three adjectives that best describe you as a qualitative researcher.
3. Create a sutra and use it in your meditation journal as a springboard for your first or an ongoing entry in your meditation journal.
4. Create a haiku about Zen.

Suggested Resources for Further Understanding

About Zen

Chodron, P. (2000). *When things fall apart: Heart advice for difficult times.* Boston: Shambala.

Hoover, T. (1980). *The Zen experience.* New York: Signet.

About Qualitative Research Methods

Pink, S. (2006). *The future of visual anthropology: Engaging the senses.* New York: Routledge.

Saldana, J. (2010). *The coding manual for qualitative researchers.* Thousand Oaks, CA: Sage.

Uhrmacher, P. B. & Matthews, J. (2005). *Intricate palette: Working the ideas of Elliot Eisner.* Upper Saddle River, NJ: Pearson.

What is the sound of one hand clapping?

Zen koan

Glossary of Terms

The terms listed in this appendix are common to practitioners of meditation, Zen Buddhism, and/or yoga. I want first, however, to say a few words about yoga, as it is closely connected with meditation. The connections are important since the Sanskrit word yoga means "union," or "yoking together," of the mind and body. For those who practice yoga there is no escaping meditation. The fact that Zen offers us a way to calm the mind and stop all noise allows for moving forward in the yoga poses, or *asanas*. Yoga is an ancient science with a long history imbedded in meditation and vice versa. This primordial method from the East offers many ways to see the Zen of qualitative research.

Here are some introductory definitions for the words used throughout this book.

Bodhisattva refers to anyone practicing meditation and Buddhism. The word is derived from the Bodhi tree where Siddhartha Guatama, Buddha, sat and attained enlightenment.

Buddha literally means "awake" and so a Buddha is an awakened one. Siddhartha Guatama was named "the awakened one" and so is called Buddha. Any awakened one is a Buddha. Buddhism is nontheistic. We all have the potential to become a Buddha with an awakened mind.

A **Chakra** is a center of energy in the body. Chakras are believed to connect to psychological properties of the mind as connected to the body. There are seven chakras and each is aligned to a part of the body. The lower chakras refer to instinct. The upper chakras refer to thinking and our mental abilities. Imagine a person seated in the lotus position of yoga, or with legs crossed. The base of the seated person is the home of the first chakra, the root chakra. Next are the sacral chakra, the navel chakra, heart chakra, throat chakra, the third eye chakra, and finally the crown chakra. One purpose of chakras is to be open to the world, so as to allow the mind to be calm and meditate. If chakras are closed, it is believed that physical ailments follow.

Contemplative inquiry is research that is designed with a deep and serious emphasis on thought and that is conducted without clutter in the mind, without clutter in design of the study, and with openness to mindfulness. Contemplative inquiry uses techniques of the qualitative research process, and it is solid in its awareness of the implications of impermanence, non-self and nirvana. It relies on intuition, creativity, and the imagination. It includes an aesthetic component such as poetry, visual arts, or digital art forms.

Dharma is that which sustains. It refers to the duty or teachings that sustain life as a whole. Dharma exists apart from humans, as opposed to a moral code, which is devised by humans. The idea of seeking understanding of dharma is related to the idea of meditation as a path to that understanding.

Japanese poetic forms are a set of artistic poetic styles, as pithy as a sutra or a koan. Early Japanese poets extolled the beauty of the natural world around them. As it always does, the poetry encompassed more than one meaning, and became a metaphor for social situations. Here in the West we are most conversant with and aware of **haiku.** This form of poetry is most often associated with Zen. Other poetic forms are described in Chapter 7.

A **Koan** is a riddle-like story that poses a question from a teacher to a student. Some Zen teachers call it a paradox. Basically, the emphasis is on meditation on the question, which is intended to allow the learner to find illumination, calm, and peace. The word koan originated from the Japananese words "ko," which means public, and "an," which means matter for thought. Probably the most famous koan is the question "What is the sound of one hand clapping?"

A **mantra** is a regularly repeated word or series of words that is spoken, sung, or chanted. Many practitioners repeat the word Om. It is believed that this word contains all the sounds of the universe and thus is perfectly suited for mantra-based meditation practice. Many spiritual traditions use the mantra-based approach. In Zen practice it is a technique for calming the mind. In one of the week-long workshops I experienced through the Chopra Center, whose staff traveled to Florida, Deepak Chopra suggested the words Ho Hum as a beginner mantra to get started with meditation. Regardless of the mantra, the aim is to still the mind and to empty it of noise and confusion.

Meditation is extended thinking, thought, or contemplation. It is calm thinking. It is a path to enlightenment, according to the Zen writers. Meditation tones the mind because it relaxes the body. I like to think of meditation as exercise for all parts of the brain.

Mindfulness is a term found in all Zen literature. Mindfulness is the goal of meditation as well as life. It is the opposite of mindless occupation with its accumulation of things, clutter, noise, and all that keeps one from being mindful.

Monkey mind refers to the mind drifting all over the place while one is trying to meditate.

Om is the universal sound syllable in meditation. It is the sound that connects the universe as one, which is the reason why it is chanted most often at the beginning and end of yoga classes. It is also chanted in meditation.

Sangha refers to the entire community of people who practice meditation through Buddhist philosophy with awareness of impermanence, non-self, and nirvana.

Satori is identified as sudden enlightenment, coming to know one's true nature, and a state of consciousness attained through intuitive illumination and practice of meditation.

A **Sutra** is a pithy bit of wisdom to teach a life lesson. In Sanskrit it literally means a thread. Many sutras are named, such as the gratitude sutra. I use sutra in this book in its broadest and most literal meaning.

Veda is a Sanskrit word meaning knowledge. It refers to the ancient texts of India and the oldest texts on the spiritual life.

Zen is a way of approaching life through meditation. It depends on learning from a teacher who has a lifetime of practice and who continually renews that practice. It is often mantra based. It is also sometimes referred to as zazen meditation, which is meditation practiced seated, facing a wall and with no distractions. Typically, and in my own practice, it includes thirty minutes of seated meditation and then thirty minutes of walking meditation. The connection to mind/body alliance is clear, which is why yoga is a perfect complement to Zen meditation. Yoga means union in Sanskrit, in this instance the union of mind and body. Zen encompasses the principles of compassion, loving kindness, and mindfulness.

Zendo refers to any formal or informal meditation space. Your own meditation area is a type of zendo.

 **APPENDIX B**

Meditation Applications

There are hundreds of meditation applications that are free or available for a small fee. This appendix is a sampler of the free applications for mobile devices such as the iPad and iPhone.

1. Relax Meditation with Zen Sounds

2. Mindful Meditation

3. Meditation Timer

4. Relax Melodies Oriental Meditation

5. Complete Relaxation Life Guided Meditation

6. Transform your Life: A Year of Awareness

7. Take a Break-Guided Meditation

8. Meditation 4 Inner Wisdom

9. Stop, Breath, and Think

10. Chakra Yoga & Meditation

11. Zazen Zen Meditation and Timer

   Buddhadarma: The Practitioner's Quarterly

A Sampler of Meditation Resource Centers

Center for Contemplative Mind in Society

www.contemplativemind.org/about

The Center for Contemplative Mind in Society transforms higher education by supporting and encouraging the use of contemplative/introspective practices and perspectives to create active learning and research environments that look deeply into experience and meaning for all in service of a more just and compassionate society. It is located in the area of Northampton, Massachusetts. The Center sustains a newsletter, webinars, annual meeting, and a journal. The Journal of Contemplative Inquiry is a new peer reviewed online journal for all who design, use, research, and access contemplative practices in post-secondary education.

Mission Dharma

www.missiondharma.org/

Mission Dharma offers retreats, programs, meditation classes and is located in the Mission district of San Francisco, California.

Spirit Rock Insight Meditation Center

www.spiritrock.org/

The Spirit Rock Insight Meditation Center offers many programs including retreats, mindfulness meditation days, meditation classes and more. It is located in West Marin, California.

The Rama Meditation Society

www.ramameditationsociety.org/

The Rama Meditation Society is a virtual center focused on teaching meditation. It is located in Scottsdale, Arizona. A complete list of activities, workshops, and classes is available on this website.

The Center for Mindful Inquiry

www.mindfulinquiry.org/index.html

The Center for Mindful Inquiry, located in Brattleboro, Vermont, is dedicated to mindfulness for professionals. The Center of Mindful Inquiry (CMI) is dedicated to teaching the practices and principles of mindfulness to professionals. CMI offers online and face-to-face courses, consultancies, and workshops for professionals who are both new to and experienced in mindfulness practices. The basis of the work is a non-sectarian approach to insight (vipassana) meditation and Buddhist philosophy, out of which all mindfulness practices grow. All courses taught at CMI integrate study, meditation, and reflection in community as vehicles for developing wise and compassionate action in the world.

The Chopra Center

www.chopra.com/

The Chopra Center is internationally known and offers many workshops at the Center in Carlsbad, California, as well as around North America and the world. It also offers webinars, online meditation classes, face-to-face yoga and meditation classes on site, and Ayurvedic training. The Chopra Center was founded in 1996 by Deepak Chopra, M.D., and David Simon, M.D., and is the premier provider of experiences, education, teacher trainings, and products that improve the health and well-being of body, mind, and spirit. The Center provides an integrative approach to total well-being through self-awareness, and through the practice of yoga, meditation, and Ayurveda. The consciousness-based teachings of Vedic science, as translated by the Center's founders, coupled with cutting edge research and modern western medicine, serve as the foundation for Chopra Center teachings. The Center collaborates with visionaries, scientists, pioneers, physicians, and industry experts to educate and inspire seekers from around the globe to better their lives and the lives of those around them.

Kripalu Center for Yoga and Health

www.kripalu.org/

This well known center located in the Berkshires of Massachusetts offers retreats, classes, teacher training, and wellness and health workshops, facilitated by a faculty from around the globe. The mission of the Center is "to empower people and communities to realize their full potential through the transformative wisdom and practice of yoga." By definition, this includes meditation, Ayurvedic medicine, and mindfulness.

Arizona Center for Integrative Medicine

integrative medicine.arizona.edu

Andrew Weil's Center for Integrative Medicine is associated with the University of Arizona; both are in the area of Tucson, Arizona. Dr. Weil's goal is to transform medicine and thus transform life. He encourages and holds workshops, conferences, etc. on integrating mind and body practices. These include meditation, yoga, and health and well being courses.

Preventive Medicine Research Institute, PMRI

www.pmri.org/dean_ornish.html

This center is located at San Francisco State University and is dedicated to health and wellness. Dean Ornish's lifetime of research is focused on health and its relationship to heart disease. His website describes the institute as a nonprofit research center investigating the effects of diet and lifestyle choices on health and disease. It also offers meditation practice as part of wellness. Dr. Ornish sponsors an ongoing web log, or blog, on these topics.

The Dzogchen Center

www.dzogchen.org/

The Dzogchen Center was founded in 1991 by Lama Surya Das after studying in Tibet for more than two decades. He is the highest ranking Tibetan Lama in North America. The Center teaches classes, holds retreats and workshops, and offers many resources for meditation. The website lists books, videos, and other resources.

A Sampler of Digital Resources for Qualitative Researchers

The following are just a few of the many online resources available for qualitative researchers.

Digitales

www.digitales.us/

This site introduces the viewer to digital storytelling in multiple formats and catalogues many such stories. By inclusion of voices there is a social justice component to many of the life histories, oral histories, and biographies.

Center for Digital Storytelling

www.storycenter.org

The Center for Digital Storytelling is dedicated to the art of personal storytelling. It offers workshops, programs, and ad services, all focused on capturing personal voice and facilitating teaching methods. The motto is: Listen deeply, tell stories.

Stories for Change

storiesforchange.net

This site is an online meeting place for community digital storytelling and advocates of social change. It is a wealth of information and offers many models of exemplary storytelling, resources and a curriculum. To use this site, you need to open an account to upload your digital stories.

Center for Studies in Oral Tradition
www.oraltradition.org
Founded in 1986 with the approval of the Board of Curators of the University of Missouri, the Center for Studies in Oral Tradition stands as a national and international focus for interdisciplinary research and scholarship on the world's oral traditions. The mission is to facilitate communication across disciplinary boundaries by creating linkages among specialists in different fields. Through its various activities the Center tries to foster conversations and exchanges about oral tradition that would not otherwise take place. It has established a series of paper and web publications aimed at serving a broad academic constituency, and it sponsors a number of events and offers bibliographic information and resources for anyone wanting to get started in oral history, life history, and archival work.

Digital Directory for Qualitative Research Resources and Websites
www.nova.edu/ssss/QR/web.html
This page on the website for *The Qualitative Report,* a peer-reviewed, online, bi-monthly journal, is the first stop for an all inclusive A-Z list of every possible resource, website, listserv, and blog related to qualitative research methodology.

Comprehensive List of Mobile Apps for Qualitative Research
www.mrmw.net/news-blogs/295-a-quick-review-of-mobile-apps-for-qualitative-research
This site is updated regularly and lists applications for qualitative research for all mobile devices.

A Sampler of Poetry Blogs

There are literally hundreds of poetry blogs for posting poetry, getting feedback and thinking in a poetic way. This list is a small sample of those sites.

Write Out Loud: Encouraging Poetry Performance
www.writeoutloud.net/
This site features news and blogs about poetry with well known and beginning poets. Reviews, publications, videos, and presentations are listed and a calendar is provided for poetry performance.

THEThe Poetry
www.thethepoetry.com/
The following statement from the website describes THEThe Poetry and the origin of its name.

> THEthe Poetry is a blog about poetics, for both poets and non-poets. It takes its name from Wallace Stevens' poem "The Man on the Dump," which ends with a question and an answer: "Where was it one first heard of the truth? The the." THEthe is a forum for ideas on poetry and the poetic aspects of fiction, non-fiction, music, visual art, film, and "the things / That are on the dump (azaleas and so on) / And those that will be (azaleas and so on)." Our contributors are writers, readers, artists, critics and so on. Our readers are writers, readers, artists, critics and so on. All are people on the dump, where "one sits and beats and old tin can, lard pail. / One beats and beats for that which one believes. / That's what one wants to get near." We hope that THEthe will help us all get a little closer.

Poets read and discuss their works online on video or in blogs.

Best New Poets

bestnewpoets.org/

This site is a blog that features fifty new poems each year and has an open forum for discussion.

The Poetry Foundation

www.poetryfoundation.org/

This site is the first stop for any aspiring poet or anyone who wants to learn more about poetry. The site features a daily poem, readings by poets, Poetry magazine, and news and items about poetry.

Poem Hunter

www.poemhunter.com/

This site is a wealth of information, and almost any poem can be found here by author, title, or topic. It also has links to other key sites. It has an open poetry forum, a calendar of poetry events, and other fine resources. It is a home base for anyone interested in poetry.

Basic Technology: Tools and Trends for Qualitative Inquiry

The NMC Horizon Project

wp.nmc.org/horizon2010/

The annual *Horizon Report* of the New Medium Consortium describes the continuing work of the NMC Horizon Project, a qualitative research project established in 2002 that identifies and describes emerging technologies likely to have a large impact on teaching, learning, or creative inquiry on college and university campuses within the next five years. Also see net.educause.edu/ir/library/pdf/HR2012.pdf

VoiceThread

voicethread.com

VoiceThread is a collaborative, multimedia slide show that is stored and accessed online. It holds images, documents, and videos and allows people to navigate pages and leave comments in five ways: using voice (with a microphone or with a telephone), text, audio file, or video (via a webcam). It is a flexible tool so it can be used for a wide variety of uses such as:

- orally publishing written work with matching art work displayed on the side,
- uploading interviews for analysis,
- describing qualitative methods and techniques in a research class,
- displaying videos for comment and feedback,
- gathering perspectives on an idea or concept from participants indicating a more active role for participants, and
- creating an archive of interview responses.

Animoto

animoto.com/

Animoto automatically produces beautifully orchestrated, completely unique video pieces from your photos, video clips and music. With this resource you will learn to make a video from your photographs. For the tutorial, see www.youtube.com/watch?v=tivxjNRFLaY, and for a sample, see www.youtube.com/watch?v=uMiws3Qq5pY. By using Animoto, the qualitative researcher starts to practice ways to merge artistic expression and the written text.

Wordle

www.wordle.net/

Using Wordle, it is possible to create a visually stunning use of word arrangements for part of the final narrative of a qualitative research project. Wordle is a tool for generating "word clouds" from text that you provide. The clouds give greater prominence to words that appear more frequently in the source text. You can tweak your clouds with different fonts, layouts, and color schemes. The images you create with Wordle are yours to use however you like. You can print them out or save them to the Wordle gallery to share with others.

Wordpress

www.wordpress.com

WordPress is an open source blog publishing application that is useful for telling a story. It features integrated link management; a search engine-friendly, clean permalink structure; and the ability to assign nested, multiple categories to articles. Also, multiple author capability is built in to the system, and there is support for tagging of posts and articles. Some researchers have made posters using Wordpress to display data at conferences and other sites. In addition, WordPress makes available to users a selection of graphics and photos.

Audacity

audacity.sourceforge.net

Audacity is a free shareware for recording and mixing audio tracks from different sources. You can download and install it from the website. Using it, you are able to capture the words of your participants in their own voice.

PhotoVoice

www.photovoice.org/

PhotoVoice is a technique used in some projects to allow participants to photograph, describe, and explain their social context, particularly groups most often on the margins of society. This project began as a way for underprivileged students and parents to use photography to capture neglect, abuse, and other aspects of the social context that give witness to the lives of those on the outskirts of society. PhotoVoice has various goals including:

- to enable an individual to keep a record and reflect a community's strengths and concerns, as, for example, shown in the photographs taken post Hurricane Katrina;
- to promote critical dialogue about community issues within a given community; and
- to eventually reach policymakers through the power of the photograph.

A growing body of PhotoVoice examples can be found on YouTube at www.youtube.com/watch?v=shrFa2c305g. Since this is a visual medium, it is helpful to view these assorted examples as models of what is possible for qualitative research projects.

Dedoose

www.dedoose.com

Dedoose is a cross platform site with multiple resources and a membership fee. It is designed to help with qualitative analysis, among other things. It offers videos, web resources, and a host of explanations for approaching analysis for a qualitative study. It also offers consultants and other resources.

An Example of a Meditation Journal Entry

This entry was written on Wed. March 21, 2007, at Ponte Vedra, Florida, during a week-long workshop hosted by the Chopra Center. Dr. David Simon was the teacher for this meditation class.

David Simon is leading the meditation today and he is using as the theme "It is what it is and will always change." There are over 250 persons in this huge hall and some are taking notes, most are sitting in seats, and some are sitting against the wall on the floor. I notice how noisy having 250 people in a room can be even though we are technically in silence before during and after the class. Coughing, sneezing, books dropping, papers rattling, outside noises, etc. Oh for some absolute silence, if there is such a thing. This is an amazing week as we are doing about three hours or more of meditation each day and about two hours of yoga. This class is scheduled for 2 hours. Our food is also in accord with ayurvedic principles so this contributes to the calm and peace of the experience. Also being here at this stunning setting, the Ponte Vedra Resort and Inn just across the road from the Atlantic Ocean, is amazing. I did not know there was an untouched beach area in Florida outside of Sanibel and Captiva Islands. Who knew that Jacksonville had so many nooks and stunning vistas! As I understand it, the yoga is optional as we are focused on meditation and mindfulness for this course. It is one of the required courses for the teacher training program at the center. David puts us all at ease and begins with us just noticing our breathing. His words of wisdom are always comforting, like "Life is a roller coaster ride so accept it and go with the flow." He gives an example used by one of his swamis (teachers), who just had a heart attack. He describes this event and how the swami maintained a happiness in his heart which helped with healing. He repeats, "Ride the wave of change, it is what it is." Then we have at least 45 minutes of silent meditation and we are asked after the class is over to go back and write about what we are learning. David always uses literary statements as well, for he closes with Emerson: "Who you are shouts so loudly in my ear, I can't hear what you are saying." Many things to think about.... Before tomorrow's session, I will have to write some thoughts out for meditation.

 **REFERENCES**

Altheide, D., Coyle, M., DeVriese, K., & Schneider, C. (2008). Emergent, qualitative document analysis. In S. N. Hesse-Biber & P. Leavy (Eds.), *Handbook of emergent methods* (pp. 127-154). New York: Guilford Press.

American Psychology Association. (2010). *Publication manual of the American Psychology Association,* (6th ed.). Washington, DC: American Psychology Association.

Barone, T. (2001). Science, art and the predispositions of educational researchers. *Educational Researcher 30*(7) 24-28.

Barone, T. (2004). Educational poetry that shakes, rocks, and rattles. *Journal of Critical Inquiry into Curriculum and Instruction, 5*(2), i.

Bochner, A. (2002). Criteria against ourselves. *Qualitative Inquiry, 6,* 278-291.

Chodron, P. (2000). *When things fall apart: Heart advice for difficult times.* Boston: Shambala.

Chopra, D. & Simon, D. (2004). *The seven spiritual laws of yoga.* New York: John Wiley.

Creswell J. W. (2013). *Qualitative inquiry & research design: Choosing among five approaches.* (3rd ed.). Thousand Oaks, CA: Sage.

Crocco, M., Lee, S., Teachers College (New York, N.Y.), Rockefeller Foundation, & HBO Documentary Films. (2007). *Teaching the levees: A curriculum for democratic dialogue and civic engagement.* New York: Teachers College Press.

Csikszentmihalyi, M. (1996). Creativity: Flow and the psychology of discovery and invention. New York: Harper.

Das, S. (1997). *Awakening the Buddha within.* New York: Broadway Books.

Das, S. (2000). *Awakening the Buddhist heart.* New York: Broadway Books.

De Felice, D. (2013). *A phenomenological study of teaching endangered languages online: Perspectives from Nahua and Mayan educators.* University of South Florida: ProQuest, UMI Dissertations publishing, 3554412.

De Mille, A. (1991). *Martha: The life and work of Martha Graham.* New York: Vintage Books.

Denzin, N. (1997). *Interpretive ethnography: Ethnographic practice in the 21st century.* Thousand Oaks, CA: Sage.

Derrida, J. (1972). *Positions.* Chicago: University of Chicago Press.

Dewey, J. (1934). *Art as experience.* New York: Minton, Balch.

Edwards, B. (1979). *Drawing on the right side of the brain.* Los Angeles: J. P. Tarcher.

Eisner, E. W. (1981). On the differences between scientific and artistic approaches to qualitative research. *Educational researcher, 10*(4), 5-9.

Eisner, E.W. (1994). *The educational imagination,* (3rd ed.). New York: Macmillan.

Eisner, E. W. (1997). *The enlightened eye: Qualitative inquiry and the enhancement of educational practice,* (2nd ed.). New York: Pearson.

Eisner, E.W. (2004). *The arts and the creation of mind.* New Haven, CT: Yale University Press.

Feldman, R. (2004). Poetic representation of data in qualitative research. *Journal of Critical Inquiry into Curriculum and Instruction, 5*(2), 10-14.

Ford, J. A. (2002). *In this very moment: A simple guide to Zen Buddhism,* (2nd Ed.). Boston, MA: Skinner House Books.

Furman, R. (2006). Poetic forms and structures in qualitative health research. *Qualitative Health Research, 16*(4), 560-566.

Goldberg, N. (2005). *Writing down the bones: Freeing the writer within.* Boston: Shambala.

Grocke, D. (2006). "Music is a moral law"–A quotation from Plato? *Voice Resources.* Retrieved January 8, 2015 from voices.no/community/?q=colgrocke061106

Hanh, T. N. (2001). *You are here: Discovering the magic of the present moment.* Boston: Shambala.

Hawkins, E. (1992). *The body is a clear place.* Princeton, NJ: Princeton Book Company.

Hesse-Biber, S. N. & Leavy, P. (2007). *Feminist research practice: A primer.* Thousand Oaks, CA: Sage.

Hoover, T. (1980). *The Zen experience.* New York: Signet.

Janesick, V. J. (2000). The choreography of qualitative research design: Minuets, improvisations and crystallization. In N. K. Denzin & Y. S. Lincoln (Eds.), *Handbook of qualitative research,* (2nd ed.). (pp. 379-399). Thousand Oaks, CA: Sage

Janesick, V. J. (2010). *Oral history for the qualitative researcher: Choreographing the story.* New York: Guilford Press.

Janesick, V. J. (2011). *Stretching exercises for qualitative researchers,* (3rd ed.). Thousand Oaks, CA: Sage.

Kapleau, P. (2000). *The three pillars of Zen: Teaching, practice, and enlightenment.* New York: Anchor Books.

Kerouac, J. (1959). *Belief & technique for modern prose.* Retrieved from writing.upen.edu/~afilreis/88/kerouac-technique.html

King, S. (2000). *On writing: A memoir of the craft.* New York: Scribner.

Kvale, S. (1996). InterViews: *An introduction to qualitative research interviewing.* Thousand Oaks, CA: Sage.

Latham, R. & Mathews, W. (Eds.). (1970). *The diary of Samuel Pepys.* Berkeley: University of California Press.

Leavy, P. (2009). *Method meets art: Arts based research practice.* New York: Guilford Press.

Lichtman, M. (Ed.). (2011). *Understanding and evaluating qualitative educational research.* Thousand Oaks, CA: Sage.

Lofland, J., Snow, D., Anderson, L., & Lofland, L. H. (2006). *Analyzing social settings: A guide to qualitative observation and analysis,* (4th ed.). Belmont, CA: Wadsworth.

Mai Mai, S. (Ed.). (1978). The *mustard seed garden of painting: A facsimile of the 1887-1888 Shanghai edition.* Princeton NJ: Princeton University Press.

Mani, V. (1975) *Puranic encyclopedia, (*1st ed.). New Delhi: Motilal Banarsidass.

Montessori, M. (2007). *The absorbent mind.* Radford, VA: Wilder Publications.

National Commission for the Protection of Human Subjects of Biomedical and Behavioral Research, (1978). Ethical principles and guidelines for research involving human subjects. The *Belmont Report.* (DHEW pub. no. OS 78-0012).Washington, DC: U.S. Government Printing Office.

Osho. (1999). *Creativity:Unleashing the forces within.* New York: St. Martin's Griffin.

Pascale, C. M. (2011). *Cartographies of knowledge: Exploring qualitative epistemologies.* Thousand Oaks, CA: Sage.

Progoff, I. (1992). *At a journal workshop: Writing to access the power of the unconscious and provoke creative ability.* Los Angeles: Jeremy P. Tarcher.

Reinharz, S. (1996). *Feminist methods in social research.* New York: Oxford University Press.

Richardson, L. (2001). Getting personal: Writing stories. *International Journal of Qualitative Studies in Education, 14*(1), 33-38.

Rubin, H. J. & Rubin, I. (2012). *Qualitative interviewing: The art of hearing data, (*3rd ed.). Thousand Oaks, CA: Sage.

Sacks, O. (1995). *An anthropologist on Mars.* New York: Alfred A. Knopf.

Saldana, J. (2010). *The coding manual for qualitative researchers.* Thousand Oaks, CA: Sage.

Sandburg, C. (1923). Poetry considered. *Atlantic Monthly.* March, 342-343.

Schiff, S. (2010) *Cleopatra: A life.* New York: Little, Brown, and Company.

Skloot, R. (2011). *The immortal life of Henrietta Lacks.* New York: Broadway Paperbacks.

Slotnick, R. (2010). *University and community college administrators' perceptions of the transfer process for underrepresented students: Analysis of policy and practice.* University of South Florida. UMI dissertation publishing, 3424385.

Stevenson, C. N. (2002). *A case study of educational leader perspectives on technology use in the undergraduate classroom.* Roosevelt University. Dissertation Abstracts. Unpublished doctoral dissertation.

St. Exupery, A. (1943). *The little prince.* New York: Houghton Mifflin.

Suzuki, S. (2011*). Zen mind, beginner's mind: Informal talks on Zen meditation practice.* (2nd ed.). Boston: Shambala Press.

Tharpe, T. (2003). *The creative habit: Learn it and use it for life.* New York: Simon & Schuster.

Tutu, D. (1999). *No future without forgiveness.* New York: Doubleday.

Venkatesh, S. (2008). *Gang leader for a day: A rogue sociologist takes to the streets.* New York: Penguin Press.

Visedo, E. (2012). *From limited English proficiency to educator: Four Spanish-English journeys.* University of South Florida. UMI Dissertation.

Watson B. (Translator). (2009). *The lotus sutra.* New York: Columbia University Press.

Willis, P. (2002). Poetry and poetics in phenomenological research. *Indo-Pacific Journal of Phenomenology, 3*(1), 1-19.

A ZEN INDEX/ZENDEX

....

It is not a question of what you do.
It is a question of how you do it.

....

....

When you listen attentively to anyone,
then you forget your self.

....

 **ABOUT THE AUTHOR**

Valerie J. Janesick, Ph.D. (Michigan State University), is Professor of Educational Leadership and Policy Studies at the University of South Florida, Tampa, where she teaches courses in Qualitative Methods, Curriculum Theory and Inquiry, and Ethics. Her research and scholarly writing focus on the use of qualitative research methods in the arts and humanities; expanding narrative inquiry through the use of poetry, video, theater, and visual and performing arts; and integrating qualitative inquiry into the understanding of critical pedagogy in the classroom. She has written numerous articles and books about subjects in these areas, including *Stretching Exercises for Qualitative Researchers* (3rd ed., 2011, Sage Publications) and *Oral History Methods for the Qualitative Researcher: Choreographing the Story* (2010, Guilford Press). In her spare time Valerie is studying to become a yoga and meditation teacher.

89603968R00104

Made in the USA
Middletown, DE
17 September 2018